It's a wonderful manual for parents of teens! I liked each chapter and the emphasis on the importance of self-soothing, the path to individuation, and becoming resilient – a key strength often lacking in our youth.

C. Claire Law, M.S., Educational Consultant
Co-Author of *Find The Perfect College for You*

Parents of adolescents, or soon-to-be-adolescents, read *An Upward Spiral,* then reread it and reread it! You'll find practical help. You'll better understand your child. You'll learn about yourself. You'll laugh. And you'll find hope for your weary hearts!

Anita K. Palmer, San Diego
Parent

An Upward Spiral tackles the serious subject of adolescent development. Written in an appealing format mixing personal vignettes and humorous drawings, the insight about how teens develop relationships, view their parents, and learn resilience is on target!

Russell Hyken, Ph.D., Ed.Sp., M.A.
Psychotherapist and Educational Diagnostician
Author of *The Parent Playbook*

An Upward Spiral is a magnificent tool in redirecting a teenager or budding young adult into self-awareness and healthy development. It is also a key tool for us as parents, giving us a deeper look into what we can learn about our own stages of development.

Denise Dryden
Integrational Coach working with parents

Rick Johnson has developed an innovative and thoroughly attainable approach for parents of teenagers. By normalizing teenage struggles as one of the stages of development parents learn that challenges are a means to a positive end.

James Meyer M.A.
Founder Meyer Education and Family Services

An Upward Spiral presents a developmental model for understanding troubled youth and includes critical guidance for parents. Rick sheds a clear light on the complicated processes within families through straightforward writing that parents will find an easy read.

Nick Hong, Ph.D.
Psychologist and Psychotherapist

AN
UPWARD
SPIRAL

A DEVELOPMENTAL APPROACH
TO PARENTING YOUR TEEN

by Rick Johnson

Dear Marjorie,
Thanks for all
you do for
families!

R.A. Johnson

afterword by Jan Johnson
Illustrated by Shane M. Morgan

Printed and bound in the United States of America
Second printing • ISBN # 1-930043-99-6
Copyright © 2015

TO ORDER ADDITIONAL COPIES OF:

AN
UPWARD
SPIRAL

A DEVELOPMENTAL APPROACH
TO PARENTING YOUR TEEN

CALL: 1-800-628-0212
ALL MAJOR CREDIT CARDS ACCEPTED

SCOTT COMPANY PUBLISHING
P.O. Box 9707
Kalispell, MT 59904
Toll Free: 1-800-628-0212
Fax: 1-406-756-0098

versations. We settled on a beautiful, wooded 550-acre parcel of land just outside Kalispell, Montana. In planning the facilities, we sought to design the campus and buildings as a place where teens could thrive in an open, inviting space that blended a holistic and unique approach with the wonders of the Montana wilderness. In recruiting board members, we chose professional leaders such as therapists, business executives and teachers; and in hiring staff we sought not only the best of the best, but people who shared our dream and commitment to teens. By early 2003, Summit Preparatory School came into being—a state-of-the-art school with an amazing facility that few can rival and a nurturing, relationship-based program that we continue to refine in striving to remain a leader in the field.

All of our efforts throughout the years at Summit Preparatory School have been based upon a specific therapeutic approach. From land procurement to campus construction, and from initial program development to daily operations, the goal has been the same—to help teens who are struggling get back on track in normal adolescent psychological and social development. A key part of these efforts entailed developing a therapeutic model to serve as the foundation of the program. To this end, Rick crafted the Summit Model with the assistance of his wife, cofounder and fellow psychotherapist, Jan Johnson. This book is based on the developmental principles that provide the foundation of the Summit Model.

Summit Preparatory School has now been in operation for over a decade with a proven track record of success. Our dream continues, and we have had the privilege of helping hundreds of teens and families. Our mission is to transform lives, and this book is also intended to support that mission. Written for parents of teens, this book is designed to help parents gain a better understanding of the developmental journey that occurs between childhood and young adulthood. If you are the parent of a teen, I hope this book helps you understand your teen better and that you find some of the book's suggestions useful.

FOREWARD

By Alex Habib

"A journey of a thousand miles begins with a single step." This quote, attributed to the ancient Chinese philosopher Lao-tzu, refers to how small beginnings can sometimes lead to big endeavors. This book reflects one such journey, one that began in 1978 when I met Rick Johnson as my freshmen college roommate. We quickly bonded, and our adventures and friendship continue to this day. During our time at college, we both majored in psychology and developed a lifelong passion for helping children and adolescents. While learning, we began to form a dream—to work together to create a program for teens. This seemed impossible at the time, but this dream was the first step in what has turned out to be a long and wonderful journey.

Following college, our lives and careers led us in different directions, but we retained our close friendship, keeping alive our shared dream. Then in 2000, Rick approached me about starting a therapeutic boarding school. He had been the administrator of psychiatric hospitals and outpatient programs, but was excited about this relatively new type of treatment program for teens. He quickly pointed out that at that time there were virtually no independent, non-profit, therapeutic boarding schools. There were even fewer with a nurturing, relationship-based clinical model designed to help teens get back on track in life. The possibilities intrigued me.

In deciding to move forward on this idea, Rick and I were soon joined by Mark Hostetter and Jan Johnson. As founders of Summit Preparatory School, we worked together to fulfill the long-standing dream born in those days of late-night dorm room con-

This book is gratefully dedicated
to all the parents and teens with whom
I have had the honor to work with and
get to know over the past thirty years.

Finally, if you are reading this book as a parent of a teen that we have served at Summit Preparatory School, it has been a privilege and a great honor to share in your journey. We value your trust and willingness to share in the dream that is Summit Preparatory School, and you have my deepest gratitude.

Alex Habib
Board Chair and Founder
Summit Preparatory School

CONTENTS

FORWARD by Alex Habib i

INTRODUCTION 1

CHAPTER ONE
ADOLESCENCE: A TIME OF CHANGE 5
Change and Adolescent Development ~ Teen Brain Development ~ Emotional versus Rational Brain ~ Brain Chemistry ~ Neurotypical and Neuroatypical Brain Development ~ Why Brains Matter ~ Personal Factors Affecting Psychosocial Development ~ No Man Ever Steps in the Same River Twice

CHAPTER TWO
THE ABILITY TO SELF-SOOTHE 29
The Nature of Meltdowns ~ The Development of Self-Soothing ~ Fostering Self-Soothing in Your Teen ~ Self-Soothing and Tolerating Structure ~ The Importance of Both Relationships and Structure

CHAPTER THREE
FORMING MEANINGFUL RELATIONSHIPS 49
Meaningful Relationships Defined ~ Meaningful Relationships Require the Ability to Self-Soothe ~ Meaningful Relationships are Learned Through Example ~ Meaningful Relationships Create a Willingness to Follow Healthy Structure ~ Responding to Unhealthy Relationships ~ Meaningful Relationships: The Foundation of Identity Development

CHAPTER FOUR
INTERNALIZING HEALTHY STRUCTURE IN LIFE 71
Identity Defined ~ Identity Development ~ Groupthink and Development ~ Group Identity: Cliques and Gangs ~ Identity Confusion in Teens ~ Information Technology and Groupthink ~ Promoting the Incorporation of Healthy Structure in Your Teen ~ The Internalization of Healthy Structure: Incomplete Without Individuation

CHAPTER FIVE

INDIVIDUATION: A DIFFERENTIATED IDENTITY......... 91

Empathy and Psychosocial Development ~ Social Empathy and Friends ~ Social Empathy and Principled Moral Development ~ Social Empathy, Individuation, and Intimacy ~ Individuation and the Family ~ Promoting Healthy Individuation in Your Child ~ To Thine Own Self Be True

CHAPTER SIX

BECOMING RESILIENT 109

Practice in Self-Soothing ~ Relational Practice ~ Practice with Healthy Structure ~ Practice with Empathy ~ Practice in Being a Leader and/or Role Model ~ Practice in Handling Entitlement ~ Practice in Rebounding from Regression ~ It's Also About You as a Parent

CHAPTER SEVEN

THE SPIRAL CONTINUES: YOUR JOURNEY AS A PARENT.... 129

Why Focus on Me? ~ Adolescence: A Time of Change for Parents Too! ~ Revisiting Your Ability to Self-Soothe ~ The Importance of Meaningful Relationships ~ The Need for Healthy Structure in Your Life ~ Reinforce Your Personal Sense of Self ~ Final Words

AFTERWORD

A DEVELOPMENTAL APPROACH TO TREATMENT AND ITS APPLICATION AT SUMMIT PREPARATORY SCHOOL......... 145

A Normalized Setting ~ Emphasis on Empathic, Meaningful Relationships ~ Healthy Structure ~ A Program Framework Based on Progressive Psychosocial Skill Development

APPENDIX

COMMON TEEN DISORDERS... 157

Drug and Alcohol Abuse and Addictions ~ Behavioral Addictions ~ Mood Disorders ~ Social Anxiety and Social Anxiety Disorder ~ Attachment Disorders ~ Learning Disabilities ~ Nonverbal Learning Disorder and Asperger's Syndrome (AKA Autism Spectrum Disorder)

BIBLIOGRAPHY.. 169

INDEX 171

ABOUT THE AUTHOR 176

INTRODUCTION

*Life is a journey up a spiral staircase; as we grow older we cover
the ground we have covered before, only higher up…*

William Butler Yeats

"My child is on a downward spiral!" Many parents express the
same fear when they see troublesome behavior emerge in their
teen. The teen may display emotional outbursts, a rise in defiance,
increased anxiety or a growing tendency to isolate from others.
Watching their teen's behavior shift so radically causes parents to
worry that their teen is becoming psychologically unstable.

Yet these behaviors are rarely because of deep-seated pathology. Instead, they occur as a result of their teen entering a new
phase of intertwined psychological and social development (or
psychosocial development). This new phase of psychosocial development often crashes down on teens with such intensity that
it causes them to revert to acting more childish, similar to how he
or she acted when younger. Because the teen appears physically
and intellectually more mature, these childish behaviors are sometimes mistaken as signs that a teen is becoming incorrigible or that
a long-term psychiatric disorder may be forming. In reality, they
most often indicate a behavioral regression to a more immature
state.

Because the same adolescent pressures that result in childish
behavior can also trigger the first behavioral signs that a psychiatric
disorder is developing, it is well worth seeking professional assistance for an evaluation. Yet given how often problematic teen behavior is related instead to psychosocial development (even when a
disorder does exists), a developmental approach to parenting teens
can prove quite effective. It allows parents of teens to recognize

1

that their child is not on a downward spiral, but instead is at the cusp of developing a new level of maturity. The immature behavior they see in their teen results from childhood skills that are not advanced enough to meet the new challenges of adolescence. This is why their teen regresses and acts more childish.

The good news is that teens do not lose these earlier skills. Instead, they revisit them, which provides the foundation for the development of more advanced skills. This reworking of past skills represents a spiral upward, where behavioral regressions indicate opportunities to promote further psychosocial maturity.

Based on this developmental understanding, this book is written for parents of teens. It is designed to provide insight into adolescent psychosocial development and to offer ideas for parents to consider in developing strategies for promoting maturity in their teen. This book is divided into seven chapters:

- Chapter One describes all the changes that teens face during adolescence that require the development of a new level of psychosocial maturity.
- Chapter Two is about self-soothing, an important foundational skill that promotes the ability to delay gratification and equips teens to cope with all the changes and stress in their life.
- Chapter Three discusses the importance of meaningful relationships to psychosocial development and how to foster the ability to form such relationships in teens.
- Chapter Four is about how teens, as part of identity development, begin to internalize structure through their identification with others. It explores how this often begins by teens mimicking peers and discusses ways to encourage teens to extend this identification to more mature individuals in internalizing healthy structure.
- Chapter Five describes the process whereby teens develop a more mature, differentiated identity—one with an individuated personal sense of self. This helps teens become less vulnerable to peer pressure and provides the foundation for further psychosocial development upon entering adulthood.

- Chapters Six is about how resiliency forms by ongoing practice in the skills previously described and especially how important it is to practice working through regressions.
- Chapter Seven returns again to the cyclical nature of psycho-social development and how parents many times experience a developmental spiral similar to their teens in revisiting and strengthening their own psychosocial skills.
- Afterword, written by my wife and cofounder Jan Johnson, explores how the developmental approach described in this book can be applied to professional treatment settings with Summit Preparatory School given as an example.
- Appendix includes a short description of common teen disorders that need to be addressed to provide a better quality of life and to assure optimum psychosocial development.

This book is based on my wife's and my experience working with teens for more than three decades across a variety of settings ranging from outpatient to inpatient and most recently as cofounders of Summit Preparatory School, a therapeutic boarding school in Kalispell, Montana. In setting out to write this book, I assumed it would be a pretty solitary process, but I found it to be more of a group process than I anticipated. So I have a number of people to thank.

First to my wife Jan, who has been my partner both in the writing of this book and in life. My gratitude can't be stated strongly enough! I love you, and don't know what I would do without you! To my parents, Wes and Carol, you have my lifelong appreciation for teaching me about good parenting through your nurturing and enduring patience. I am truly blessed to be your son. To Alex Habib and Mark Hostetter, dear friends whose ongoing support and commitment to teens and families has made all this possible. I can never thank you enough! And Alex, thanks for thirty-five years of friendship, and here's to 35 more! I love you, my friend. To Barb Cunningham, for your patience in reading earlier versions of this book and the hours spent helping to edit it—my deepest appreciation, and Go Griz! Thanks also to Liann Ainsworth for your feedback and encouragement. And my sincere thanks to Todd Fiske for your friendship and dedicated leadership at Summit Prep. I also want to thank the students and parents who have been a part of Summit Prep throughout the last decade. You have taught me so much, and being a part of your lives has been truly an honor. And finally to my children, Sarah and Rachel, who have been a joy. You bring light to your mom's and my life, you have our love and deepest affection, and we will always cherish our relationship.

CHAPTER ONE

ADOLESCENCE: A TIME OF CHANGE

Nothing endures but change.

Heraclitus (c. 535 – c. 475 BCE)

I can still vividly remember the warm spring day when we brought our first child home from the hospital. It was a short drive along a familiar route, yet this time it felt much different. This time we were coming home with a baby girl, and we were her parents! We knew having a baby would change our lives, but my wife, Jan, and I felt ready for these changes. We had stocked the house with all the requisite baby gear and made sure our child development textbooks were within easy reach on our bookshelf. As trained psychotherapists, we had learned in graduate school that children progress through predictable stages of development so we assumed that we knew exactly what to expect.

As time went on, we found that our daughter's development did follow a fairly predictable progression throughout her childhood. Despite the predictability, we still found a few surprises along the way. For the most part these were fun surprises, such as her first word being "cow" instead of "dada" or "mama," her resistance to our attempts to tame her wild curly hair, and her determination to wear her Halloween bat costume all year round. We found these quirky traits endearing. So it was with minimal concern that we watched as she progressed psychologically and socially seemingly right on schedule. She was a fun, loving child with close emotional ties to her family. She grew into a bright, creative young girl who did pretty well both academically and socially. Then she became a teenager.

Our daughter Sarah, Age 5

While we were ready for some of the changes adolescence brought, our daughter started to surprise us in ways for which we just weren't prepared. Many of these changes weren't the fun kind of surprises we had come to appreciate. Her fashion sense shifted from no-fuss to overdone. At times, we also noticed new words in her vocabulary, but these were less cute accompanied with an unpleasant tone. While she was still a joy, at times she also seemed to be regressing in becoming less confident, less able to make mature decisions, and even less trustworthy. We had anticipated bumps along the way, but some of these surprises seemed to indicate that she was becoming less mature psychologically and socially—that she was actually losing ground developmentally. What was happening? These behaviors seemed so out of character for her.

If you are the parent of a teenager, perhaps your experience is similar to ours. The child you thought you knew so well suddenly at times seems to be a different person. Your bright-eyed, outgoing, cute little child overnight reverts to an anxious adolescent prone to immature behavior and mood swings. Perhaps your teen has also become untrustworthy, demanding, and argumentative. Maybe your teen has begun to withdraw from family and friends or shows a strong, sometimes desperate desire to always be with

"I don't think the term
Sweet Sixteen applies."

a certain group of peers, Your teen may even change his or her physical appearance in order to fit in. What's happening?

To understand better what is happening to your teen, consider for a minute that life for all of us entails an ongoing series of transformations. Our bodies and brains morph with age. Our mental capacities expand along with our understanding of the world. Our relationship with our family of origin changes. Our social networks and relationships expand and contract. Our roles and responsibilities begin to alter. All of these transformations happen while the societal and cultural world around us is in constant flux. In order to thrive amid all this dynamic activity, we each need to learn to identify and adjust to change psychologically, socially and emotionally. This process involves recurring cycles where one's psychological and social skills are repeatedly revisited and strengthened throughout life. These cycles are often preceded by a temporary lapse into less mature behavior caused by existing skills proving inadequate. If this cyclical process follows a positive path, or in other words an upward spiral, it is called psychosocial maturity.

The experience of change, and the need to adapt to change, is particularly intense during adolescence. This is why your teen acts in such a confusing, immature manner. As a parent myself, I can relate to the bewilderment and sense of being overwhelmed that this can bring. Our daughter is now a self-assured, competent and successful adult who is married with a child of her own. Like the rest of us, she continues to revisit her skills to strengthen them in response to new twists and turns in life, which she handles well as an adult. Getting to adulthood, however, was a struggle at times, especially during her teen years.

So let's untangle the course of adolescent development and examine why these struggles occur. I will suggest ways to promote healthy growth and maturity in your child. I will use the phrase "psychosocial development" to describe the spiral whereby teens revisit and strengthen key intertwined psychological and social skills in becoming more mature. But let's begin by reviewing all the changes that occur in the life of a teen and how this affects adolescent development.

Change and Adolescent Development

Young children develop physically through a series of fairly predictable stages. They learn first to roll over, crawl, then walk, before learning to run. Similarly, psychosocial development in childhood also progresses through a gradual series of stages, where skills build one upon another. However, once a child reaches adolescence, this progression isn't nearly so straightforward. The slow, methodical process of skill development in childhood can't keep up with the fast-paced, complex changes that occur in the life of teens. While childhood skills provide the foundation for further development, they are not sufficient to meet the ever-increasing challenges that teens face. When these skills prove inadequate, teens tend to regress and act more impulsive and immature. This helps explain why teens sometimes appear to be headed in the wrong direction developmentally.

As a result, teenagers need to revisit their childhood psychosocial skills in strengthening and expanding upon them. This abrupt need to update these skills occurs due to the sheer volume of physical, emotional, psychological and social changes that teens experience. Puberty begins to reshape a teen's body from that of a child toward one of a young adult. Acne may sprout on a once baby-smooth face. Concerns may surface about one's physical development as compared to peers. New feelings of sexual attraction begin to emerge. Adolescence also brings with it the tendency for mood swings and extreme emotional states, and a teen's capacity for abstract thinking expands. Socially, a teen begins to experience more intense group and social pressures than ever before.

If you asked your teen to share honestly what the experience of all these changes is like, the response might be something like this: "I feel as if I have the weight of the world on my shoulders. My body is morphing into something different, and my skin is breaking out. I can't get to sleep at night, and then can't seem to get up in the morning. I have feelings and urges I just don't know what to do with. My emotions seem to be on an endless roller coaster

The Teenage Experience

ride, and I struggle for a sense of direction. And on top of it all, I feel like I'm in one of those terrible dreams about being on stage, in my underwear, with all my flaws on display to be judged by my parents and laughed at by my peers!"

It is no wonder your teen may struggle given all that is going on in his or her life! And this is what we call normal teenage stress, something all teens experience to one degree or another. The sheer volume and intensity of all these changes can't help but frequently overwhelm the psychosocial skills that your teen developed during childhood. And the changes don't end there.

Teen Brain Development

It was once believed that brain development was finished by the time a person becomes a teenager. But it isn't! We now know that there are substantial changes in brain development that occur during adolescence and continue into young adulthood. Brain development actually intensifies during adolescence as part of the physical changes that occur during the shift from childhood to adulthood. This brain expansion is similar to what occurs during the period of time known as the terrible twos, the transitional period from infancy to toddler when a child experiences a significant boost in self-awareness, language capacity and physical coordination.

You can compare these changes in a teen's brain to a computer upgrade that allows the brain to become faster and more efficient. This involves several physical modifications. Let's look at two.

The first is an upgrade to the wiring through an increase in white brain matter (myelin). This provides better insulation and connections in the wiring in the brain. It also significantly speeds up the transmission of electrical impulses.

The second is a decrease in the volume and connections within the brain's grey matter (neurons). This occurs through a pruning process where connections that are not regularly used are gradually eliminated. It is similar to reducing the number of unused programs running on a computer to increase its processing efficiency. While this primarily clears childhood brain clutter, pruning can also reduce brain connections related to healthy behavior if these pathways are never used.

Emotional versus Rational Brain

Teens often respond more emotionally than rationally. To understand why we must start with the brain. The brain contains many structures. Let's take a look at four main ones:

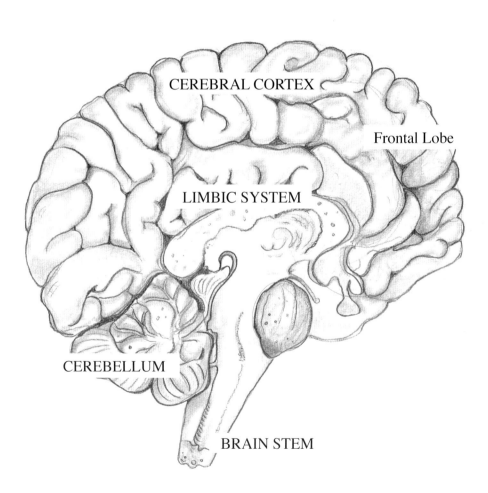

1. **The Brain Stem** is responsible for basic survival including heart rate, breathing and digestion.
2. **The Cerebellum** controls automatic reflexes and muscle coordination.
3. **The Limbic System** is an interconnected set of brain structures responsible for emotions. It is often called the emotional brain.
4. **The Cerebral Cortex** is comprised of four lobes that perform higher brain functions. The frontal lobe manages thinking, planning, reasoning and decision-making. It is often called the rational brain.

The development of each of these sections of the brain occurs at different rates during adolescence. In general, growth occurs first at the back of the brain and moves forward (left to right on the illustration). It also starts at the bottom of the brain and moves upward. This means that the frontal lobe is the final section to fully mature. Since the brain's frontal lobe is the rational portion controlling the ability to reason, information received by the brain will be interpreted by your teen's limbic system or emotional brain first until the frontal lobe catches up. Thus, you can expect your teen's responses in many situations to appear more emotional than rational. Have you ever experienced anything resembling the following conversation?

"Mary, you have a big test coming up tomorrow. I think you should stop texting your friends and study."

"But I like my friends!"

"This isn't about your friends. It's about needing to study."

"What's wrong with my friends?"

"Your friends are fine—it's just that you got a D on the last test, so you should really study more for this test, okay?"

"So now you're saying I'm stupid!"

"No, you are a bright girl who just needs to apply herself better."

"Great! My own mother thinks I'm stupid!"

These sorts of bewildering exchanges can catch many parents

off guard. It seems the more you try to use logic and reasoning to resolve a situation, the more illogical and emotionally charged the situation becomes! This disconnect occurs because your attempts to address your teen's rational brain are instead being interpreted by your teen's emotional brain. This is why it may feel like a short-circuited conversation, it is because your teen's frontal lobe is still developing. Any wonder communicating is sometimes difficult? At these moments, it is best just to empathize with your teen, while following through on any necessary limits or consequences, instead of trying to have a logical conversation. It is much better to wait until your teen has once again calmed down enough to use his or her frontal lobe before attempting to have a productive conversation.

Brain Chemistry

In addition to changes in the wiring and rate of brain development, there are also changes in the levels of important chemicals in the brain that can affect teen behavior. Some of the most well known of these chemicals are testosterone and estrogen, often referred to as sex hormones. Many parents are aware that an increase in sex hormones will trigger physical changes in their teen. What they may not realize is that these hormonal shifts can also affect a teen's mood. Testosterone interacts with the fight-or-flight section of the brain. It can make teens, especially boys, more prone to irritability and outbursts of anger or aggression. Estrogen, on the other hand, appears to affect the levels of chemicals in the brain that help regulate mood, which may make teen girls more prone to moodiness and feelings of sadness.

Changes in the level of other brain chemicals called neurotransmitters can also influence teen behavior. Neurotransmitters allow nerve cells to send and receive messages. When the levels of neurotransmitters are not in proper balance, this information may become scrambled. This can result in difficulties in such areas as mood and attention.

Many factors affect the level of neurotransmitters in teens, and a change in the level of these chemical messengers can alter how a teen feels and behaves. To understand this better, let's look more closely at three key neurotransmitters: norepinephrine, dopamine, and serotonin.

Norepinephrine is a neurotransmitter that triggers the brain's fight-or-flight response in times of perceived threat. It affects the parts of the brain where attention and reactions to stress are controlled. Changes in the level of this neurotransmitter can influence mood, including making depression and anxiety worse. For some teens it may also be a factor in struggles with attention and focus.

Dopamine is a neurotransmitter that, among other things, affects a person's experience of pleasure. In general, an increase in dopamine causes an increase in feelings of pleasure. Researchers have found that changes occurring in the adolescent brain can cause a temporary increase in teens' sensitivity to dopamine. The result is an escalation in their tendency to seek immediate, constant, pleasurable, and rewarding experiences. In other words, experiences that increase dopamine. Because the frontal lobe is still under construction, this sensation-seeking behavior is not adequately tempered by rational thought. Sensation-seeking behavior tends to cause teens to increase their participation in risky behaviors without considering the potential consequences. If your teen seems easily bored, constantly seeks increased excitement, seems to be taking foolish risks, and is difficult to please, brain chemistry may be a factor.

Dopamine also plays a significant role in drug and alcohol abuse and addiction. Drugs and alcohol can elevate dopamine levels far more than most natural pleasurable experiences. With regular use, the brain eventually begins to equate pleasure with these higher levels of dopamine. As a result, activities that used to be experienced as pleasurable no longer produce the same effect. When this occurs, teens begin to increasingly seek these artificial highs and may use drugs or alcohol to try to enhance activities that used to be enjoyed sober. These behaviors can rapidly lead to abuse of drugs or alcohol, even when negative consequences occur. For some teens, this can also lead to addiction. Addictions develop when teens become physically and psychologically dependent on drugs or alcohol as a part of daily functioning in order to feel normal. Choosing to avoid use is then no longer an option. Because teens tend to seek the experience of increased dopamine, the risk of abuse and addiction is higher for teens than for adults.

Serotonin is a neurotransmitter that helps regulate mood. A shortage of serotonin in the brain can contribute to moodiness, impulsiveness, and in some cases depression. If your teen experiences a change in serotonin levels—not uncommon during adolescence—this may cause difficulties with mood and increase impulsive behavior. So if you believe your teen is experiencing persistent, debilitating depression or anxiety, serotonin levels may be a factor. If you are at all concerned about your teen's moods, seriously consider consulting a psychiatrist regarding the potential benefits of medication and counseling.

Neurotypical and Neuroatypical Brain Development

So far we have examined the brain development of normal or average teens, described in scientific terms as neurotypical. However, please note that every teen is unique and wired differently, even within the parameters of what is considered neurotypical. For example, some teens are wired more as introverts, while others as extroverts. Some are wired as higher risk-takers, while others as lower risk-takers. Some are wired with greater emotional variability, while others with less. Brain wiring also affects how flexible or rigid a teen tends to think and act. Brain wiring even affects reasoning and social ability, which varies across neurotypical brain development.

The level of variation in brain development can also fall outside the norm. This is called neuroatypical. This term can apply both to being gifted, such as being smarter than the norm, or to having certain behavioral or intellectual deficits relative to the norm. If these deficits result in significant struggles, they are often diagnosed as a learning, behavioral or psychiatric disorder. (*Note: Nonverbal Learning Disorders and Asperger's Syndrome are both related to neuroatypical brain development, see Appendix: Common Teen Disorders for more information*).

Why Brains Matter

Understanding how your teenager is wired can help you find ways to respond more effectively. For example, your teen may be wired to be more rigid in his or her thinking, and adults may misinterpret this inflexibility as defiance. If this is the case and you misperceive your teen's rigidness as defiance, you might become just as inflexible as your teen in how you respond. This response can establish a destructive, punishing stalemate that unintentionally reinforces more cognitive rigidity and defiance in your teen. With a deeper understanding of your teen's brain, you can respond instead in ways that support and teach increased mental flexibility. Instead, try giving your teen choices within acceptable parameters and time to reflect upon a course of action.

Understanding that your teen's brain is still developing can also reinforce your resolve as a parent. Brain research demonstrates that the teenage brain is much more malleable—like Silly Putty® or Play-Doh®—than that of an adult. This is because teens can create new brain connections more quickly and much more efficiently than adults. These new brain connections are formed as teens practice new behaviors and learn new skills. So time spent fostering healthy behavior patterns in your teen is time well spent because you are encouraging the development of new brain connections.

Personal Factors Affecting Psychosocial Development

Teenagers experience tremendous physical, emotional and social changes, but there are other factors that can also shape psychosocial development. For example, my own children were impacted by the frequent moves our family made as they were growing up. We lived in five different cities in three different states during their early childhood. While these normal life transitions were good for our careers, they created stress in the family as we each learned to cope in our own way with all the changes we were experiencing. Your child may have had similar experiences or have been affected by other factors. Being aware of these factors can give you an important perspective, which will allow you to respond more effectively as a parent.

Although we can't examine every factor, let's take a look in detail at several common personal factors that affect teens: traumatic events, social awkwardness, being bullied, family conflicts, severe medical conditions with themselves or family members, and experiencing a psychiatric, behavioral, addictive, or learning disorder.

Traumatic Events

Trauma refers to highly stressful events occurring outside the usual realm of a teen's experience and ability to cope. Trauma undermines one of the core tasks of psychosocial development, which entails the formation of trusting relationships that allow children and teens to feel safe enough to begin to explore the world as part of developing new social and psychological skills and strengths. Trauma can also trigger a loss of faith in the safety and predictability of the world, causing self-confidence to erode. The erosion of self-confidence can have a very debilitating effect on a teen's ability to self-soothe and regulate emotions. This may adversely affect relationships and cause a teen to isolate. Trauma can also result in excessive feelings of fear, panic, anxiety and depression.

Many types of events can prove traumatic. They can include serious injury, natural disasters, divorce, sometimes adoption, the death of someone close, witnessing extreme violence, and physical, sexual, or emotional abuse. Unless the trauma is adequately addressed, further psychosocial development can become delayed or halted.

If your child has experienced trauma, be willing to listen. Many times out of your own anxiety or impatience, you may be tempted to respond too quickly with advice, such as "You need to get over this." Your teen needs to know that you understand, have the patience to accept his or her experience, and will support him or her in working through the effects of trauma. Also, strongly consider finding a therapist or a support group for people who have experienced trauma. These resources can be invaluable in helping your teen cope and heal from trauma.

Social Awkwardness or the Out-of-the-Box Teen

Teen culture tends to define successful teens as outgoing, Hollywood attractive, socially adept, trendy, and talented in a manner admired by peers (e.g. a football star). With these traits, teens are allowed to join one of the desirable cliques within the teen social hierarchy. However, most teens don't fit this definition, and many deviate to the point where they feel different than many of their peers. These out-of-the-box teens may not excel in cool activities as defined by peers. They may be slower in their physical development. They may be naturally shy and introverted. Their interests may differ from the typical adolescent culture. They may look or dress differently. They also may act awkward in social settings. Other reasons may also contribute to a teen being out-of-the-box. In the majority of these situations, if these teens have a supportive family, and at least some close friends, they survive high school and continue on to thrive as adults. Ironically, some of the traits that may make them feel so out-of-the-box in high school often become advantages later in life.

Problems can arise, however, when teens begin to feel too ostracized because of their differences. If this is occurring with your teen, you can help. Begin by empathizing with his or her struggles. Provide parental guidance regarding ways to improve social interactions, and seek social opportunities that better fit the personality and interests of your teen. If the situation doesn't improve, consider finding a therapist. A therapist can provide your teen with emotional support and can help foster improvements in your teen's social skills. A therapist can also give you advice on how to provide encouragement and guidance to your teen. In addition, through an evaluation a therapist can also help determine if a mood, learning, or behavioral disorder exists for which your teen could benefit from professional assistance (see *Appendix: Common Teen Disorders* for more information).

Being Bullied

Bullying occurs when a teen, or group of teens, use physical strength or social influence to intimidate or berate others. The reasons for bullying vary. Sometimes teens bully for the immature feelings of superiority gained by exerting power over another person. This is typically a factor in physical bullying. It is also frequently a factor in cyberbullying, including anonymous cyberbullying. When multiple teens collectively bully, they affirm their identification with a certain social group, achieved by immaturely debasing a teen that doesn't belong. Whatever the reasons, being the recipient of bullying can be quite traumatic. This is intensified if the teen is ridiculed for being noticeably different from peers, or if the teen already struggles with social awkwardness or social anxiety. Cyberbullying can increase this traumatic effect exponentially as it extends personal attacks beyond the confines of a particular setting; instead, the public humiliation broadens within the larger world of social media. This is especially insidious when it reaches the teen in his or her own home, undermining home as a safe haven. If bullying continues, over time it can affect a teen's ability to self-soothe, drain the teen's sense of self-worth, and trigger despair.

If your child is experiencing bullying, empathize with his or her struggles. If your teen seems down or depressed, consider counseling. In addition, recognize that bullying is not a normal teen conflict. Bullying involves an unhealthy, unequal distribution of power, where there is little room for negotiation and compromise. For this reason, if bullying behavior is prolonged or extreme, don't expect your teen to work it out; outside intervention is necessary. In facilitating this intervention, it will be the most effective if it addresses not only the bully, but also your child's needs and the social setting where the bullying takes place.

Family Conflict

Children need to develop a sense of security in order to feel self-assured enough to venture out into the world. Toddlers and young children routinely need to check in with a parent to make sure all is okay; this allows the child to confidently return to activities apart from the parent. Even the experience of physical and emotional pain is in part determined by this relationship. Many parents have experienced a young child who, after falling down, turns to see how his or her parent will respond before knowing if the fall was serious enough to require crying and comforting. This need for security begins in infancy, continues throughout adolescence and extends into young adulthood. Even when teens seem to push parents away, they still need to know that their parents are there for them in order to feel secure. Conflict in the family—especially chronic, unresolved conflict—is destructive and erodes this sense of having a secure base.

Destructive conflict does not refer to the temporary conflict that occurs when teens react to consequences they dislike or when they test parental limits in trying their wings. A certain amount of temporary conflict is expected. It is even healthy if it leads to a resolution and clears the air. Destructive conflict refers to chronic, reproachful exchanges based on blaming and debasing one another. This occurs when one member of the family believes the other person's behavior is belittling or malicious and responds in a spiteful manner in return. This can lead to an escalation of personal attacks and misunderstandings—such that even when the actions

of one person are not intended as a personal slight, the actions are still interpreted as a slight. This needn't even be open conflict. Sometimes subtle comments create destructive conflicts that simmer and grow beneath the surface.

If chronic conflict is present in your family, consider its effects not only on the quality of your own life, but also on the psychosocial development of your child. Destructive conflict may erode the quality of family connections and make your child feel emotionally unsafe. This may be compounded if there is any pressure to take sides in a conflict between two parents, as neither choice feels safe because it means upsetting the other parent. This takes a toll on your child's sense of security in the family. Feeling insecure within the family may result in your child being overly tentative and clingy or defiant in a desire to escape the tension and conflict. Seek to resolve this conflict, and consider counseling. If you're divorced, this includes resolving any conflict that may exist between you and your ex-spouse, especially if it is related to parenting. The spousal relationship may be irreconcilable, but any work done to make the parenting approach more united will have a positive impact over time on your child's psychosocial development. Whatever the source of the conflict don't let arguing, back biting, and insults become the norm for how people are treated in your family.

A Chronic or Inhibiting Medical Condition

Being physically independent builds confidence and lays the foundation for the development of a healthy personal sense of self. For many teens participating in certain activities such as athletics or musical performances can further reinforce self-confidence. A chronic medical condition can undermine self-sufficiency, and an injury or physical illness can inhibit participation in beloved activities that teens use to help define who they are. This is the case, for example, with teen athletes who are no longer able to participate in sports. As a result, these teens can struggle with figuring out how to become their own person—especially given the constant reminders of their physical dependency or their inability to participate in a defining activity.

These physical limitations can cause feelings of helplessness in teens. Their life feels out of their control. In addition, there are other social and emotional ramifications. For example, injured athletes no longer receive the social recognition they once enjoyed. They may be ignored by their former teammates and may lose the opportunity to strive for future goals in life such as obtaining an athletic award or a college scholarship for sports. This loss of social recognition can lead to despair and isolation, or defiance in attempting to take back a feeling of control, or to gravitating towards a negative group of peers.

Similarly, teens with a chronic medical condition may be left out of social functions, be made fun of by peers because they seem different, and may struggle with planning for the future because they feel so dependent upon others. The result can be an overreliance on others beyond what the medical condition requires. Conversely, they may also use the medical condition itself to try to show autonomy, such as a diabetic teen refusing insulin.

If your child has either a chronic medical condition or an injury affecting his or her ability to participate in a defining physical activity, provide empathy and support in helping your teen accept the condition. Then, encourage your teen to find positive options in life that are still open to him or her. Look for activities that reinforce a sense of competency and individuality. If a chronic or long-term medical condition exists, also encourage him or her to become gradually more involved in self-care. The more self-sufficient your teen can safely become the better. This support can be more effective if it includes providing accurate information about the condition, and if you allow your teen to make choices about treatment options that he or she demonstrates enough maturity to handle.

Finally, the social ramifications of either of these physical limitations need to be mitigated. So specifically plan opportunities that strengthen existing peer relationships, and that also support the formation of new relationships. This may include encouraging your teen to expand his or her social activities into areas previously unexplored. If your teen has a chronic medical condition, support groups for teens with chronic illness can also be quite helpful in gaining emotional support and knowledge from others who share the same experience.

Having a Family Member with a Chronic Illness or Disability

Having a family member with a chronic illness or disability can also affect a teen's psychosocial development. For some teens this can result in pulling away from the family prematurely, as the attention in the family is placed elsewhere. For others, it may result in being so focused on the family that attending to one's own needs is difficult.

For example, in my own family, our younger daughter is a beautiful and kind young lady with a positive spirit. She also has autism. Even though my wife and I tried our best to give equal time and attention to both our children as they grew up, our younger daughter always seemed to require more due to her disability. Our younger daughter also relied on her big sister for help in navigating the world, particularly in finding protection from the taunts of other children. Over time, our older daughter inevitably became her younger sister's co-caretaker along with us. Even by age five, she was adept at calmly soothing her younger sister's distress when teachers and babysitters couldn't. Our older daughter learned great patience and compassion in the process, traits she demonstrates today with her own child. But she also had to learn to focus on herself. Being a caretaker for a family member can make it difficult for a teen to begin to act autonomously in forming his or her own personal sense of self. The desire for autonomy conflicts with the natural pull to be with, and to assist, the ill or disabled family member. This can be especially challenging if the ill or disabled family member is the teen's primary caretaking parent or guardian.

If a member of your family has a chronic illness or disability, help your teen learn to balance his or her own needs with the needs of the family, including the ill or disabled family member. Your teen needs permission from you to have a sense of self beyond the role of being a child or sibling of an ill or disabled family member—without feeling disloyal. If your teen has become distant from the family in reaction to the situation, this permission needs to be balanced with realistic expectations for continued involvement with the family. Receiving support by peers in similar situations, such as involvement in a support group for teens with an ill or disabled family member, can help your child feel more normal by recognizing that he or she is not alone in this experience. Striving to find the right balance between personal needs and the needs of the family is difficult for a teen in this situation, but it is worth the effort. Fortunately, my older daughter found this balance. She can now look back positively at what she learned through this experience.

Psychiatric, Behavioral, Addictive, or Learning Disorders

All teens are prone to mood swings and behavioral inconsistencies. However, if a teen has a psychiatric, behavioral, or addictive disorder, these emotional and behavioral struggles can become much more intense, longer lasting, and debilitating. Teens with a learning disorder can also significantly struggle—not only with schoolwork, but also with social skills. Learning difficulties that impede the processing of academic information can also hamper managing the information necessary for effective interpersonal communication. In addition, a learning disorder can affect self-esteem as it can make even a very bright teen feel quite stupid. Any of these psychiatric, behavioral, addictive, or learning disorders may adversely affect psychosocial development. If you are concerned or have questions about your child's mental health, behavior, substance use, or learning patterns, it is advisable to seek professional help. This may include consulting a psychiatrist, a therapist, or an addiction counselor, and perhaps requesting academic and psychological testing at your child's school (see *Appendix: Common Teen Disorders* for more information).

No Man Ever Steps in the Same River Twice

"No man ever steps in the same river twice." The ancient Greek philosopher Heraclitus spoke of the inevitability of change in the context of a river, which is always flowing and changing! Although Heraclitus was speaking philosophically, change is also the basis of psychosocial development. Our lives entail an endless cycle of change from birth to our inevitable demise. We evolve physically, cognitively, emotionally, and psychologically—all the while experiencing ongoing shifts within our social and family life. Our grand task is to learn how to adapt and thrive within these changes. To do so, we must ever expand upon our psychosocial skills and thereby grow as healthy individuals able to maintain satisfying social and intimate relationships. Then, in turn, we need to help our children learn to do this as well!

In supporting your child growing up, you may have felt better prepared to understand and anticipate his or her needs as a younger child because the developmental stages of childhood typically advance in a fairly predictable progression. During adolescence, there is often a break in this pattern, and teens may appear temporarily to lose ground developmentally. Don't panic! Adolescence is not as confusing and unpredictable as it may initially appear. There is a way forward. The immature behaviors you see in your teen are a result of childhood skills that are not advanced enough to meet the new challenges of adolescence. This is why your teen seems to be regressing and acting more childish.

Your teen needs to embrace change in reworking and extending these childhood skills, a progressive process that forms an upward spiral in increasing maturity. This includes developing a more advanced sense of identity. In describing each of these skills and their related developmental stages, I will offer parenting strategies you can use to foster positive development in your child and will share tips for navigating regressions and continuing to support your own growth. To help reintroduce clarity and order, I will present teen psychosocial development as a series of four stages that build one upon another. Let's move on into examining **1) the ability to self-soothe, 2) the ability to form meaningful relationships, 3) the internalization of healthy structure in life, and 4) individuation, the development of a differentiated identity.**

CHAPTER TWO

THE ABILITY TO SELF-SOOTHE

It is in the nature of all passionate and uncontrolled emotion
to prey upon and weaken the forces of reflective power.

Elizabeth Stuart Phelps

Slammed doors. Tearful bouts over seemingly trivial matters. Withdrawal into isolation in her room. Angry outbursts. Ever since Amelia became a teenager, her parents were perplexed by their daughter's behavior. They knew their daughter wasn't a bad person. They could still sometimes glimpse the girl they knew so well behind her prickly facade. But why was she so moody and at times so hot-tempered? Why did she also tend to behave repeatedly in such impulsive, self-defeating ways, even when she knew the resulting consequences were likely to be quite serious? She just didn't seem to care in the moment. Even the deep regret she felt later failed to alter her behavior.

If you recognize any of Amelia's traits in your child, your teen's emotional volatility and impulsive behavior are likely fueled by all the physical, psychological, cognitive, and social changes that occur during adolescence. The intensity of these changes has simply overwhelmed existing self-soothing skills, which in turn has caused your teen's behavior to regress and become more childish. This intensity can also make it even harder for your teen to utilize effectively his or her still developing frontal lobe (or rational brain). When the intensity of the changes overwhelms your teen, the result is impulsivity and the tendency to react emotionally instead of rationally.

These immature emotional responses can be triggered for a number of reasons: when a desire is not immediately met, when feeling insulted or criticized, when experiencing behavioral limits or consequences, or when overexcited. These powerful emotional reactions trigger impulsive, often irrational behavior—especially if not tempered by self-soothing.

But what is self-soothing? It is the ability to keep strong emotions and impulses in check by being able to calm and reassure oneself.

So how strong can these emotional impulses be? Can they really short-circuit rational thought? Consider the example of road rage. Road rage is a situation in which many adults lose the ability to self-soothe. Here is a common scenario: Larry is driving home from work, when suddenly he needs to slam on the brakes because someone cut him off. Larry had time to avoid an accident, but still he reacts by yelling obscenities, honking the horn furiously, and trying to figure out some form of retaliation. Larry is in the midst of road rage, unable to self-soothe strong emotions. Just like Elvis, rational consideration has left the building.

Road rage is an example of an intense emotional state that short-circuits reason—unless pacified through self-soothing. Now, imagine walking around with that same level of emotion just below the surface, ready to overwhelm you at the slightest provocation. This is what your teen many times experiences: an intense, overpowering well of emotions that comes to the surface when he or she becomes angry, upset, or over-excited. When these emotions overwhelm your teen's sense of reason, impulsive behavior is the result. The most detrimental types of impulsive behaviors are meltdowns.

The Nature of Meltdowns

All adults have times when self-soothing falters and they overreact under stress and respond in ways of which they are not proud. These isolated incidents, or mini-meltdowns, are not what I am

Larry attempts to ease the
stress of his commute.

defining as teen meltdowns in this book. Instead the meltdowns I am referring to are active ongoing **patterns** of childish and destructive behaviors that occur when self-soothing skills prove habitually inadequate. To better understand, consider the analogy of a nuclear meltdown.

Nuclear power plants create electricity through generators driven by the steam produced from the heat of sustained nuclear reactions. Sometimes too much heat is created, but a nuclear meltdown only occurs if the cooling efforts fail, thereby allowing a pattern of out-of-control, degenerative, nuclear reactions akin to what occurred at Chernobyl or Three Mile Island. Similarly in teens, if self-soothing inadequately cools emotional heat, over time this can lead to patterns of increasingly regressive and impulsive behaviors. These behavioral meltdown patterns are usually self-defeating and can also have a devastating effect on the other people in the life of teens.

Even though meltdowns are destructive, in most cases that is not the intent. Meltdown patterns are most often childish, impulsive, and ultimately detrimental attempts at self-protection. The intent of teens is not to self-destruct, but to survive difficult, overwhelming situations and emotions. For example, teen drug abuse can be a result of self-medicating, a behavior teens may resort to in the absence of more mature ways of handling stress and anxiety. Another example is teens that are habitually isolative, not because of a desire to have no social life, but due to a lack of more advanced self-soothing skills in the face of social stressors. These teens immaturely act like a turtle that pulls into its shell to protect itself from the elements.

Teen meltdowns usually involve a pattern of regressive, unsuccessful attempts to handle pain, stress, anxiety, and feeling out of control. Meltdown patterns are unique to each teen, but in general can be grouped into three categories: avoidance, fight, or flight. See if you recognize any of these in your child.

Avoidance: This happens when teens try to cope immaturely by avoiding situations where distressing emotions occur. Have you noticed any of these avoidance examples occurring with your teen?

- Refusing to go to school due to emotional distress, which may appear as anxiety or apathy.
- Chronic physical complaints and illnesses with no apparent medical cause, resulting in an inability to participate in anxiety-provoking activities.
- No self-motivation to take on more advanced responsibilities in life or to try new things, which may appear as helplessness, despair, or an unwillingness to participate because of a lack of interest.
- No desire to take on age-appropriate social risks, such as dating and going to social events with other teens.
- Excessive use of computer, gaming, and social media to avoid having to socialize and participate in the real world.
- Isolation from either friends, family, or both. This tendency to isolate may include everyone, but also may be limited to new social situations and to forming new friends.

Fight: When emotions become too difficult to handle internally, teens can sometimes attempt to fight these emotions through external means. This often takes the form of childishly blaming others for their struggles and how they feel, and then battling with these people in an attempt to take control and thereby conquer these distressing emotions. You may see some of these fight responses in your teen:

- Targeted angry outbursts against those they blame for how they feel.
- Overt defiance against parental and other adult authority.
- Passive-aggressive behavior, often paired with avoidance. In these situations defiance is more covert and is demonstrated through procrastination or repeated failures to do what was agreed upon.

- Stealing just to get away with it.
- Purposely failing in school to demonstrate to parents and others that you can't make me get good grades.
- Running away to demonstrate noncompliance to behavioral limits or consequences.
- Bullying and controlling others through intimidation. This occurs frequently with peers, but can also include teens' attempts to coerce or intimidate their parents.

Flight: These are regressive attempts by teens to escape from distressing emotions, or to lessen their intensity. Note these examples of flight:

- Drug use, done not to emulate peers or to experience intense dopamine highs, but to reduce negative emotions. Some teens rely on substances to make it through stressful situations, such as taking a test, participating in an anxiety provoking social situation, or even just going to school.
- Cutting, or other acts of self-injury. This is not suicidal behavior, but a primitive and visceral attempt to release tension, anger, or other difficult emotions. This behavior provides emotional relief from a number of factors. It can make the teen feel more in control by deliberately causing the pain they are experiencing. It also induces a release of endorphins, replaces emotional numbness with intense physical sensations, and causes the teen to focus on physical pain instead of overwhelming emotional pain.
- Throwing or hitting objects, such as punching a wall. This is aggressive behavior not directed at a person, but against a handy object. The action releases distressing emotions by physically getting them out.
- Eating to self-medicate and relieve stress. Emotional eating is fairly common because food is typically equated with nurturing. On a very basic level, eating can temporarily replace emotional pain or anxiety with physical comfort and a sense of

well-being.

- Running away. Previously mentioned as a fight response, running away can also be a flight response. This occurs when a teen becomes so overwhelmed by a situation that he or she runs away to escape the strong emotions the situation evokes.

Do you recognize any of the avoidance, fight, or flight behaviors in your teen? If so, does more than one apply? Multiple types of meltdown behaviors can be common because avoidance, fight, and flight behaviors are not mutually exclusive. Teens can display a combination of different types of meltdown patterns depending upon the circumstances. For example, a teen that frequently tends to blame others as a fight response, may at times also exhibit an avoidant response by acting aloof. An anxious, avoidant teen that refuses to go to school may also exhibit the flight response of cutting to escape intense emotions.

If your child is displaying any of these regressive, meltdown patterns, it is helpful to remember that underdeveloped self-soothing skills are largely to blame. Without this understanding, you may be tempted to perceive your teen as pathologically irrational, selfish, bad, and unlikely to change. If so, you may have the tendency to respond in anger or despair. Realizing instead that this childish behavior is a result of immature psychosocial skills means that change is possible. The possibility of change instills hope. Instead of feeling disheartened, you can focus positively on the future by supporting your teen in revisiting the psychosocial skills used effectively in childhood. Helping your teen strengthen and expand these skills promotes an upward spiral in his or her overall level of maturity.

The Development of Self-Soothing

Why is self-soothing so important? Being able to calm strong emotions allows teens to delay gratification long enough to consider options and weigh the potential consequences of various behaviors **before** deciding how to act, instead of just acting on impulse. Self-soothing also helps provide teens the emotional fortitude to act upon these decisions, even in anxiety-provoking or emotionally charged situations. This includes the wherewithal to deliberately choose to act more mature in situations that previously used to trigger impulsive meltdown patterns and having the emotional strength to follow through.

The development of self-soothing begins in infancy. Although its formation is affected by inborn factors, self-soothing is primarily learned behavior. It is initially based on the sense of security children develop through their interactions with primary caregivers. If these relationships are nurturing, and caregivers predictably and reliably meet the child's needs, the child develops trust and a sense of security. When children learn that they can trust and rely on these important relationships for nurturing and protection, children tend to be less anxious and better prepared emotionally to handle daily life. Over time, with consistency and repetition, the security this secure base provides begins to become internalized, which enables children to hold onto these feelings of security in the physical absence of important caretaking adults for longer and longer periods time.

Young children tend to use a tangible reminder of their secure base in the physical absence of these adults. These tangible reminders are called transitional objects, such as a teddy bear or a favorite blanket. These objects help children transition from needing to have these caretaking adults physically present in order to feel secure to relying instead on a tangible reminder of this feeling of safety in their absence. This is an important step towards internalizing a secure base.

As their world expands, children must develop a greater ability to self-soothe. This occurs slowly as parents and other important adults introduce additional intellectual, emotional, and social challenges based upon a particular child's age and maturity level. One of these challenges involves the gradual expansion of the structure children experience in life. Structure includes the perspectives used to evaluate if an experience is positive or negative and the parameters used to determine how to act towards oneself and others. For children, their experience of structure begins externally as their parents guide their behavior by prohibiting inappropriate or unsafe behaviors and encouraging positive behaviors.

As childhood challenges progressively increase—including the need to meet the behavioral expectations of parents and caregivers—children can lapse into disobedience, temper tantrums, and emotional distress. This requires ongoing patience and understanding on the part of caregivers in reinforcing their child's secure base while continuing to uphold appropriate behavioral expectations. This remains a fairly gradual process throughout childhood, as children slowly learn to face more challenges successfully by increasing their ability to self-soothe through internalizing the sense of security that a secure base provides. This increased internalization also results in the gradual decrease in the use of childhood transitional objects. The previously beloved and relied upon teddy bear or blanket eventually becomes relegated more and more to the closet or as a decoration on the bed. Then comes adolescence!

During adolescence, a sharp spike replaces the gradual developmental slope of childhood. Teens are suddenly expected to handle more adult-level challenges and responsibilities while simultaneously experiencing immense physical, emotional, psychological, and social changes. As a result, childhood self-soothing skills are inadequate to handle it all, and teens revert to more immature behaviors and ways of self-soothing. Teens, therefore, need to revisit and expand upon existing self-soothing skills while learning new skills that allow them to better meet the challenges of rapidly approaching adulthood. Childhood self-soothing skills, including reverting back to the use of transitional objects, are just not enough to meet the demands of life as an adult.

So how are these important skills developed at a more mature level? It should come as no surprise that fostering more advanced self-soothing in adolescents involves primarily the same factors that support its initial development in childhood. It takes nurtur-

"Buttercup"
The secret of Genghis Khan's success.

ing relationships that effectively meet the physical and emotional needs of teens. As in childhood, this combination of nurturance and attention to the needs of teens again reinforces their sense of having an emotional anchor or a secure base. Through a secure base, teens develop and internalize the sense of reassurance necessary to engage more maturely with the world, even in the midst of the chaos of adolescence, without melting down and reverting to patterns of impulsive, emotion-driven behavior.

Providing teens with a secure base can be a challenge. First, the sheer volume of changes in teens' lives can be overwhelming, which can cause teens to focus more inwardly on themselves. This inward shift occurs due to the natural tendency to focus on self-protection when feeling threatened, related to one's survival instinct. When this occurs, the tendency is for teens to become self-absorbed, which places great stress on the relationships that provide teens with their secure base. Teens can become prickly, self-centered, or isolative. These behaviors can make maintaining a close relationship with them difficult.

The secure base teens experience with their parents can be destabilized further by societal and peer messages that imply that teens should be completely self-reliant and not need their parents. As a result, instead of following their parents' guidance, teens often feel they should adopt instead the perspectives and behaviors of their peers. While teens do need to begin to establish their own routines and behaviors, this pressure can push teens to attempt to take too much control prematurely over their lives—more control than they are ready to handle. This, combined with their own developing sense of autonomy, can make teens feel inadequate about relying so much on their parents. The belief that they shouldn't rely on their parents causes them to withdraw from or push parents away. Even teens that retain a close relationship with their parents can sometimes feel this tension.

Another challenge comes from the fact that the secure base achieved in childhood needs constant reinforcement during adolescence. Reinforcing a teen's secure base can be difficult for parents and other caregiving adults as often their focus becomes so fixed on a teen's behavior that the need to reaffirm the relationship is overlooked. This is understandable because the stakes are usually much higher. Toddler temper tantrums seem minor compared to immature meltdowns by teens that sometimes result in truly dangerous or scary behavior such as self-harm, running away, aggression, or drug use. These dangerous threats can make it difficult for parents and other adults to empathize with the strong emotions underlying these behaviors. Instead, the focus becomes just on stopping these alarming behaviors.

Due to the challenges, the secure base teens require to self-soothe may become wobbly at the very moment when the sheer volume of changes teens face are enough to overwhelm them. As a result, teens may no longer feel secure and trusting of the world. Their tendency to experience meltdowns due to an inability to cope then increases. When this occurs, teens need the opportunity to rebuild their emotional anchor by beginning to trust others enough to accept assistance during emotionally challenging situations. This includes accepting support and counsel in working through meltdowns when they can't adequately cope. The ability to self-soothe and delay gratification is developed within these trusting relationships. Eventually, these trusting relationships renew within teens their sense of having a secure base and in turn provide the corresponding realization that they can face strong emotions and challenging situations. As their ability to self-soothe and handle anxiety increases, impulsive behavior and immature meltdowns lessen both in frequency and intensity.

Fostering Self-Soothing in Your Teen

Based upon a developmental understanding of an adolescent's need for a secure base, fostering self-soothing begins by reinforcing your relationship with your teen. Even though the parental relationship may be stressed, your relationship remains the primary source of your teen's sense of security in life. So continually invest time and energy into your relationship, even when your teen seems to be emotionally distant. Take an interest in your teen's life and accomplishments, be willing to listen and seek activities you can do together. Your efforts may seem to go unnoticed, but these efforts will have a cumulative positive effect.

In reaffirming your relationship, make sure this includes times separate from when you need to set limits or give consequences. If the majority of time spent together is only focused on poor behavior, your teen may quickly feel you disapprove of or reject them. Remember to recognize and celebrate the achievements of your teen, as recognizing even small successes helps build the relationship on a note of acceptance and encouragement. When you need to impart limits and consequences, make sure to keep it as predictable and consistent as possible, as knowing what to reliably expect can reduce anxiety in your teen.

In supporting your child's secure base, also remember that at times it is difficult for teens to reach out to their parents. This is a normal phase for many teens. So beyond your parent-child relationship, also seek opportunities to foster relationships between your teen and other mentoring adults such as coaches, teachers, and youth group leaders. If he or she seems unwilling to form relationships with these adults, consider finding a therapist who specializes in working with adolescents. While friends can meet a portion of your teen's relational needs, peer relationships alone are usually not enough as peers often wrestle with the same struggles. Relationships with other trustworthy, nurturing adults that provide guidance and act as a role models can often better meet these relational needs and can reinforce your teen's secure base. These relationships can be beneficial even if your teen still maintains a close relationship with you. The experience provides positive modeling and reinforcement beyond the family in building healthy self-confidence in your teen.

Just as with younger children, maintaining a secure-base is also dependent upon meeting the needs of your teen in a predicable, reliable, and age-appropriate fashion. This, of course, looks different from how you used to attend to these needs during childhood because your teen should now gradually take on more responsibility for self-care. But the principle remains the same. Your teen must know that you are there to rely upon in helping meet the needs he or she is not yet equipped to handle.

As part of encouraging the development of healthy internal structure, maintain nurturing routines and interactions within your family that also reinforce your teen's secure base. These positive family routines provide a positive experience for your teen to draw upon and incorporate in life as your teen someday starts a family of his or her own. For instance, having regular meals together beyond just the holidays can provide an opportunity for family members to interact and touch base. But the success of this tactic relies on your vigilance in preventing intrusions such as phone calls, texts, or television.

While self-soothing is grounded in the experience of having a secure base, there are other activities you can encourage your teen to engage in to strengthen this skill. Learning physical relaxation techniques, exercising, or meditating can promote self-soothing. Healthy recreation also supports self-soothing. Consider ways of advancing participation by your teen in such leisure activities as sports, art, music, cooking, dance, crafts, hiking, or reading. Be willing to join in these activities. Finally, there are therapeutic approaches designed to help teach people how to regulate their emotions. If this is an area of particular difficulty for your teen or you, consider finding a therapist.

Self-Soothing and Tolerating Structure

Children and teens begin to develop their own perspectives and behavioral standards by incorporating aspects of the structure they experience with others including: the structure their parents provide through encouragement, limits, and consequences, and now also the perspectives and behaviors they experience with their friends. At times these conflict. Parents hope that the structure

The New American Thanksgiving...

(not quite a Norman Rockwell moment)

they provide will have a greater influence on their child than the perspectives and behavioral standards of negative peers and the larger world. The goal of parental structure is to promote the internalization of mature decision-making—for their teen to learn to think through potential consequences before acting, and then to display good judgment in choosing a positive course of action.

How teens initially react to parental structure often mirrors their earlier childhood reactions. Initially in both instances, parents often find that the necessary limits they impose on their child or teen's behavior meets with a strong response. For example, when parents must inhibit a young child from impulsively running into the street, the child may respond with a temper tantrum. Parents must be willing to impose this limit in spite the tantrum for the sake of their child. Teaching the child to choose without parental intervention to avoid running into the street takes time and effort. This is accomplished first through parental support given when the limit is imposed that helps the child self-soothe, which gradually helps reduce temper tantrums and allows the child to tolerate the limit better. When this occurs the child becomes more willing to abide by parental requests. Further parental encouragement begins to reinforce a desire in the child to want to follow and understand the request. Eventually, the pattern leads to the child personally choosing to follow safer ways to cross the street even when parents are absent. In this way, the child internalizes healthy structure related to crossing the street, a concept that hopefully generalizes to other potentially dangerous situations that the child might face.

Similarly, before your teen is able to begin to internalize healthy structure, you need to impose age-appropriate limits on immature behaviors despite their protests. You must require your teen to act more mature as a collaborative, participating member of the family household. For example, parents need to require the completion of reasonable chores around the house even if teens argue against this. In addition, if your teen tends to be avoidant or anxious, gradually expect and encourage your teen to maturely face stressful social situations.

Your teen will likely struggle at times with the behavioral expectations and limits you impose. For more defiant teens this is because these tend to interfere with the desire to act impulsively and to do whatever he or she wants to do. For more avoidant teens, it requires facing situations that are outside his of her comfort zone. Similar to the process with younger children, an important part of providing such structure is helping your teen learn how to tolerate this more advanced external structure without meltdowns. This means supporting your teen's ability to self-soothe by providing empathy and relational support when upholding behavioral expectations and giving consequences.

This takes patience and fortitude as a parent because the first step in your teen developing more mature and healthier structure is just learning to **tolerate** these expectations. Seeing value in and internalizing healthy behavioral expectations and limits comes later. This is important to understand, because without it you may have premature expectations, which can cause discouragement at your teen's attitude.

Why it is important to recognize that toleration comes first? Let me give you an example from the comedy movie *The Break-Up*. In the movie, the female lead character (Jennifer Aniston) tells her immature boyfriend (Vince Vaughn) that she doesn't just want him to do the dishes, rather she wants him to **want** do the dishes. Her intent is clear. As a gesture of his affection and a sign that he is ready for a more mature relationship, she would like him to do a task he finds distasteful. Her hopes are dashed when her request goes unrequited. "Now why would I want to do dishes?" her boyfriend insensitively responds. For her boyfriend, putting aside personal desires by tolerating an unpleasant task because of his affection for her is behavior he still is incapable of showing. In fact, even tolerating doing dishes for any reason seems beyond him. His response is painfully immature, which is intended as comedy for the movie audience. She is very discouraged.

Similarly, the first step in the process for teens is to learn to tolerate externally imposed parental structure through self-soothing.

"She expects me to **want** to do the dishes.
Why would I ever **want** to do the dishes???"

This includes the expectation to act mature even when to do so requires controlling impulses or responses to emotional stress. It begins with toleration. Seeing any value in acting mature comes later. In other words, teens need to be able to tolerate doing the dishes before they can begin to become willing to do the dishes. Understanding that your teen must first learn to tolerate healthy structure, before beginning to see any value in acting on this structure, will save parental disappointment. Understanding the importance of toleration as a first step will also allow you to recognize progress in your child.

The Importance of Both Relationships and Structure

This chapter began by examining self-soothing and how it is fostered through a secure base established by nurturing relationships that also meet the physical and emotional needs of teens. Developing the ability to self-soothe through these relationships allows teens to take the first step towards eventually internalizing healthy structure—which is the capacity to tolerate externally imposed behavioral expectations. This demonstrates the importance of providing both supportive relationships and external structure to teens. One without the other is not enough. Parental structure that is provided devoid of a secure, meaningful, parental relationship is less likely to be tolerated and ultimately internalized. A parental relationship that provides no structure does not foster the development of maturity in teens.

In our discussions regarding the need for both structure and relationships, so far I have primarily focused on how they affect your teen. However, their importance also applies to you as a parent. In regards to structure, practice what you preach. You need to live by similar behavioral expectations and limits on immature behavior that you are working to instill in your teen. In doing so, you reinforce healthy behavior in yourself, and you also serve as a good role model. This doesn't mean that you need to live with the exact same rules, such as curfew. But rather that you demonstrate the level of personal maturity that goes along with these extended adult privileges. The principal of acquiring more autonomy because one is more emotionally mature—not just older—is one you need to live by.

In regards to relationships, you also need to have the relational support necessary to self-soothe. With this in mind, you must work on your own relationships to find the support you require. Reinforcing your relationships increases your ability to self-soothe. In turn, that makes you a more relaxed individual while helping you respond more effectively as a parent. When your teen loses his or her cool, it is not the time for you to lose yours too! Instead, strive to be emotionally healthy enough to consistently role model effective self-soothing. Show your teen that you can emotionally handle his or her immaturity. Your empathic patience in imparting structure, without overreacting, builds a sense of trust and security. It gives your teen the important message that you are willing to be there, even at his or her lowest.

Finally, the importance of relationships and structure resonate throughout all stages of your teen's maturation. Effectively balancing these two components is crucial to ongoing psychosocial development. So let's move on to next explore the qualities within relationships that can best promote healthy psychosocial development in your teen.

CHAPTER THREE

THE ABILITY TO FORM MEANINGFUL RELATIONSHIPS

Friendship is essentially a partnership.

Aristotle (c. 384 – c. 322 BCE)

Recently I spoke at a parent support group, which was followed by an informal coffee hour. Each of the parents had a story to tell about their own child. As they took turns sharing, four different scenarios emerged:

- Ryan's parents described how Ryan used to be very close to them. They smiled when they reminisced about how in grade school he always came to them for reassurance after a tough day in school and sought their advice on just about everything. But now he seemed so distant, choosing to be with his friends instead of family and avoiding coming home unless absolutely necessary. The only time he spoke to them was when he wanted money, food, or a ride to social activity.

- A single mother expressed concern about her daughter Julie's relationship with her boyfriend. Since Julie started dating Bill, she seemed to become so immersed in the relationship that not much else mattered. Julie changed everything from her hairstyle to her choice in music in order to match Bill's preferences and stopped hanging out with her girlfriends. Her mom found out that Julie had phoned Bill's weekend employer, at Bill's request, to lie about his absence one Saturday morning claiming it was due to the flu instead of a hangover. She also discovered that this wasn't the first time Julie had made excuses for Bill's irresponsible behavior. Julie's mom shared that Bill often seemed overcritical of Julie, which made her wonder if her daughter was being treated with appropriate respect. When she tried to talk to her daughter about her relationship with Bill, Julie turned quite defensive and angrily stormed out of the room.

- Sophie's parents shared their apprehension about their daughter's choice of friends. These girls were quite demanding in what they expected from members of their group: from wearing the right designer clothes, to going to all the right parties, to making sure each member acted appropriately condescending to uncool peers. There was also competition for social status among the girls within their own group, resulting in significant drama. Sophie's parents reported seeing firsthand how gossip and power struggles seemed more the norm than kindness and real friendship.

- Mike's parents seemed a bit hesitant to talk at first. They claimed that Mike had never been a behavior problem and that they had a great relationship with him. Eventually, the mother's eyes filled with tears. She shared how worried she was about their son's social life. Mike just seemed out of his element in high school. To make matters worse, his peers often teased him about his social awkwardness, and this was affecting his self-esteem. Mike had also stopped participating in activities he used to enjoy and chose to isolate more and more—even from old friends he had known for years.

As each parent shared, the other parents expressed their mutual support and provided suggestions. At one point during the discussion, I raised the question whether or not their children shared anything in common? Each teen's situation seemed so different from the others that at first this seemed unlikely. But then, almost simultaneously, the parents recognized a common denominator—relationships. Each of their teens seemed to lack positive sustaining relationships. Ryan's former close relationship with his parents was now quite distant and self-serving. Julie sacrificed friendships with girlfriends, and her own likes and dislikes, in order to maintain a relationship with a boy. Sophie complied with a group of peers that seemed more concerned with competing for social standing than with friendship. Mike struggled with forming new connections and maintaining friends. In each case, there was something about the relationships of each of these teens that appeared to be having a significant negative effect on their lives.

While relationships and structure are important to the psychosocial development of teens, in many ways relationships come first. Through relationships, initially with primary caregivers, children and teens experience the nurturance and responsiveness necessary for self-soothing. Relationships also provide the backdrop for experiencing structure in the form of behavioral expectations one is expected to adopt. This includes both parental expectations and peer expectations. The importance and the quality of these relationships affect how willing the teen is to accept and abide by their expectations. So before I discuss how a teen begins to internalize these expectations in the form of internal structure, I will focus on relationships.

In the examples of Ryan, Julie, Sophie, and Mike, their relationships, or lack thereof, are adversely affecting their development. For everyone except Mike, these relationships seem to demonstrate a certain degree of emotional closeness. But they lack the qualities that bring out the best in each of these teens. Instead, these relationships reinforce immaturity. Developing the types of relationships that do promote maturity requires a level of abstract reasoning, personal introspection, and morality beyond the capacity of most young children. Adolescents are at the cusp of being able to form such connections—ones that promote positive personal growth and maturity. I label these as meaningful to distinguish them from casual acquaintances, or from the types of unhealthy or immature relationships we will examine later. Before we look at how teens develop the ability to form such relationships, let's begin by defining what makes relationships meaningful.

Meaningful Relationships Defined

Meaningful relationships are those that promote personal growth and support the formation of a mature personal sense of self. These self-affirming connections over time tend to have a greater and more positive influence on the life of teens than any other type of relationship. They can even outweigh the pull of negative peer pressure. This is why the ability to form meaningful relationships is so important to teens.

What are the qualities of meaningful relationships? One important quality is authenticity. Relationships are authentic when they are based upon a mutual, realistic understanding and acceptance of one another. This allows each person to be real and to feel accepted, without having to pretend to be someone else in an effort to retain the connection. This may seem a simple concept, but authenticity requires the openness to accept others for who they are and the courage to be oneself within the relationship.

Meaningful relationships are also those that demonstrate cooperation, compromise, and reciprocity based upon the motivation to understand and respond to the other person's needs. They require simultaneously considering one's own needs and desires along with the needs of the other person, giving both equal importance. Meaningful relationships require a more advanced level of abstract reasoning, where multiple perspectives can be examined at the same time. They also require the inclination to act thoughtfully towards others based on this new understanding. Prior to meaningful relationships, children may place their own needs second for the sake of others. But often this altruistic behavior is due either to a desire to gain a reward or to the level of rudimentary empathy many children develop that includes a natural tendency to want to please others. Neither represents weighing simultaneously what is in the best interest of both the other person and oneself in choosing a course of action.

When teens become increasingly able to consider the needs of others along with their own and become willing to act on behalf of others, they also begin to demonstrate the qualities of cooperation, compromise, and reciprocity. These qualities represent an advancement in moral development, from pre-conventional to conventional. Pre-conventional morality involves actions taken just to avoid punishment or to seek a reward. Conventional morality entails also considering the effect one's actions have on others. Ethically, the perspective shifts from actions based solely on the external motivators of rewards and punishments to actions based also on a thoughtful internal consideration of the needs of others in choosing how to behave.

Considering the needs of others also requires making the effort to **listen** to others in order to grasp the significance of what is being said. Listening means attending to what others are really saying without allowing distractions to interfere and without immediately trying to interject or counter. Listening is a hallmark of meaningful relationships. However, listening takes ongoing work on the part of each member in the relationship. After all, how many adults can say honestly that they never let their own self-serving desires interfere with listening to an important person in their life?

The ability to form meaningful relationships means teens also need to recognize and associate with others who are just as committed to authenticity, cooperation, mutual benefit, and compromise. Seeking out others committed to the same qualities allows teens to form relationships that exhibit a healthy balance of power. A healthy power balance exists when each member is committed to assuring mutual benefit for one another. These relationships are partnerships in which decisions that affect both members are made conjointly. Within meaningful relationships, each member receives comparable recognition and encouragement. In addition, coercion is kept to a minimum, and neither partner is abusive.

"I know, no one listens to your needs, so...
Do you need me to finish that for you?"

Meaningful Relationships
Require the Ability to Self-Soothe

The development of meaningful relationships, with the qualities mentioned above, requires a more advanced level of cognitive and intellectual development than most children possess. Increased cognitive ability comes with adolescence. But younger children can show many of these qualities within relationships too. This is based both on a younger child's level of reasoning and also on his or her ability to self-soothe. For younger children, learning to self-soothe allows for more mature interactions and relationships.

The ability to self-soothe, and hence delay gratification, allows children to become better able to follow social rules, such as sharing. Self-soothing also allows children to begin to focus beyond themselves in forming attachments with others beyond their primary caregivers. This forms the basis for children to begin to want to understand what others are thinking and feeling, which is a precursor to cooperation, kindness, and the establishment of elementary empathy. These relationships are important to psychosocial development and provide the foundation for many qualities of meaningful relationships. However, they still tend to focus largely on the child getting his or her own needs met within the relationship. These altruistic behaviors—the need to please others and to make them happy—do not typically reflect the relational depth and complexity of true mutuality found in meaningful relationships.

Promoting the ability to form meaningful relationships in teens builds upon these earlier childhood skills. Forming meaningful relationships for a teen is also linked to their ability to self-soothe. When a teen's self-soothing skills prove inadequate to meet the challenges of adolescence, their behavior regresses including towards others. Behavioral regressions prevent the further development of relationship skills, often also resulting in a lapse in the childhood skills already developed. Fortunately, as teens learn to self-soothe at a more advanced level, they revisit childhood relational skills and strengthen and expand upon them. Combined with advances in abstract reasoning that allow teens to consider multiple perspectives simultaneously, more advanced self-soothing skills sets the stage for teens to develop the capacity to form deeper more meaningful relationships. Given the right circumstances, the result is an upward spiral in psychosocial development that allows teens to focus genuinely on authenticity, mutual benefit, and reciprocity within relationships.

Learning more advanced self-soothing also allows teens to avoid, or recover from, two common relational pitfalls that interfere with the formation of meaningful relationships. The first is the previously mentioned tendency to be too self-absorbed. Becoming too self-absorbed is a self-protective impulse that occurs when teens feel overwhelmed due to struggles with self-soothing. Becoming overly self-absorbed can impede focusing much beyond the confines of their own immediate needs. The result is behavior that becomes increasingly self-centered. Teens don't choose to be selfish. But their ability to consider the needs of others has been eclipsed by their own needs. Their seemingly narcissistic behavior comes from this self-protective impulse.

In contrast, struggles with self-soothing can also result in becoming overly self-effacing. This can include the tendency to discount the value of their own needs and often to avoid any social recognition because they don't feel proud of themselves. This happens when teens become overwhelmed by negative input about who they are or by perceived failures in their life. These feelings can erode their self-esteem. Instead of becoming self-absorbed, they tend to deny their own personal needs, which can lead to a level of self-denial or even self-loathing.

Neither being self-absorbed or overly self-effacing allows for the formation of meaningful relationships. One reason is that both of these traits make authenticity next to impossible. Being self-absorbed makes it hard for teens to be authentic, as authenticity is incompatible with their single-minded self-centered behavior. Others are perceived to be there only to serve the needs of the teens, not to have needs of their own. In contrast, being overly self-effacing can also cause teens difficulty in being authentic with others, as they tend to hide themselves out of shame. These teens believe others' needs and interests are what's really of value, not their own.

A teen's ability to listen and respond to others also requires the ability to self-soothe. Truly listening and attending to others' needs—a quality crucial to meaningful relationships—is difficult for teens that become self-absorbed due to struggles with self-soothing. As a result, these teens often end up inattentive to others' needs and overly demanding in regards to their own needs. This results in an unhealthy balance of power within the relationship, where the overly demanding teen's needs take precedence.

In regards to power, teens that are overly self-effacing and dis-count the importance of their own needs find themselves in the opposite position within relationships. Again, an inequitable bal-ance of power exists, but for these teens the other person gets the majority of the attention. In turn, the self-effacing teen experi-ences a lack of control in the relationship. This may not be im-mediately obvious. But look at the disproportionate influence the other person's approval or disapproval has on a more self-effacing teen's self-esteem. Look also at how much the other person's needs and opinions dictate the teen's decisions. Again, reciprocity and mutual benefit within the relationship are lacking.

What are the implications? In promoting the important abil-ity to form meaningful relationships, the first step is to reinforce your teen's ability to self-soothe. I encourage you to review tactics previously discussed for reinforcing self-soothing in your teen. Im-proving skills at self-soothing allows your teen to access childhood relational skills once again in strengthening and adding to these skills. Improving self-soothing sets the stage for further advance-ment in developing the ability to form meaningful relationships. Based on this foundation, the next step is to introduce the qualities that comprise meaningful relationships to your teen, qualities that are best learned through example.

Meaningful Relationships
Are Learned through Example

The capacity to understand and then express the qualities that comprise meaningful relationships is not innate. While the capacity builds upon earlier childhood relational skills, it requires the ability to care for others with the same degree of personal attention and understanding one has for oneself. Prerequisites for this skill include an increase in abstract reasoning and the ability to self-soothe. But no surprise: this important relational ability is only learned within relationships.

This means that your teen needs opportunities to experience the qualities of meaningful relationships firsthand from others. This experience is about quality, not quantity. Even one meaningful relationship can outweigh the effect of multiple other affiliations in life. This is demonstrated by how often adults talk about how a key person had such a positive impact on them growing up, much more so than other friends or acquaintances. What typically made such an impact? These individuals demonstrated the qualities of meaningful relationships.

While as a parent you can be such a person to your teen, let's first see how you can seek opportunities for your teen to meet others who are psychologically and emotionally mature enough to demonstrate these qualities. These are often the same people who display the patience and maturity to reinforce self-soothing in your teen as mentioned in Chapter Two. Perhaps you have a relative or family friend that your teen seems to gravitate towards—one who routinely displays these positive relational qualities. Find ways to encourage these relationships. Include these people in family activities, or allow your teen to participate in social activities with these individuals: a sporting event, a church/synagogue activity, or involvement in a hobby they both enjoy such as fishing or biking. If your teen resists these suggestions, consider finding a therapist who works with adolescents using a more relationship-base approach. Within these relationships, your teen will have the opportunity to experience positive recognition, encouragement, and support. Experiencing these qualities will foster a desire to reciprocate. Over time, this reinforces your teen's ability to form more meaningful relationships.

In seeking opportunities for your teen to experience these qualities, don't forget yourself! Displaying these qualities with your teen is imperative. Your relationship remains your teen's most important source of emotional anchoring as his or her secure base. As such, your relationship will continue to have a great impact on your teen's psychosocial development. For a young adult, this includes learning how to have more mature relationships.

As a parent, believing in the importance of your relationship may be difficult if your teen is like Ryan, the boy who withdrew from his parents. Perhaps like Ryan, your teen has also pushed you away in a premature attempt to become more autonomous. Ryan also displays a common phenomenon, an increased demand for physical support from his parents with seemingly little gratitude. Demanding support without gratitude occurs when teens feel threatened by any emotional expression of needing their parents. So instead of asking for emotional support, they seek reassurance through material goods and physical support. Of course, showing gratitude also feels like a threat to their autonomy. Therefore, they seldom express "thank you." Despite displaying behavior that seems to imply otherwise, teens need to retain a sense of having a secure base with their parents. If your teen acts like this, remember that your relationship does matter—even if at times your teen seems more interested in what you can do for them materially.

Whether your child is similar to Ryan or not, you remain very influential in your teen's life. This extends beyond just providing a secure base. The qualities you demonstrate provide one of the most important sources for your teen to draw upon in learning to form more meaningful relationships. For this reason, consider how best to demonstrate within your relationship the qualities of reciprocity, a healthy balance of power, and authenticity.

Reciprocity means a willingness to return in kind an action that

"Sure we're still close, Dad!
I come to you all the time...
for money."

benefits you with an action that benefits the other person. With this definition in mind, seek opportunities to plant the seeds of reciprocity whenever you can. When someone does something nice for you or your teen, help him or her understand that the best response is thankfulness, and to return the kindness. When you make sacrifices for your teen, consider verbalizing that you are putting your own needs second in the situation. Then, without imposing guilt, ask him or her to consider responding in kind in the future. Also, find activities that you can do together for the sake of someone else. Look for a friend in need or opportunities to volunteer within the local community. This helps reinforce the growing tendency in your teen to reciprocate by participating with you in giving back to others.

The balance of power is trickier. Of necessity, you need to retain parental authority within the relationship. This may make some parents uncomfortable when their teen accuses them of being on a power trip. But as the parent of a teen, your obligation is to retain authority in implementing appropriate limits and consequences throughout the teen years. You can't abandon this responsibility. But retaining authority doesn't mean using a dictatorial approach. Instead, authority should be expressed in a more supportive and collaborative fashion. Demonstrate a healthy balance of power by being careful to avoid misuse of your authority just to meet your own needs. You can also grant your teen increasing opportunities to make decisions that he or she demonstrates enough maturity to handle. Reinforce the skills further by negotiating or compromising on certain limits when your teen shows enough maturity to abide by whatever is decided. Allowing fair and age-appropriate compromises demonstrates that limits are intended to encourage maturity rather than to unfairly inhibit teens from enjoying life.

Authenticity is another important quality to reinforce in your relationship. Fostering authenticity means you truly listen and accept your teen for who he or she is. Don't ignore behavioral issues or forego future dreams, but love and accept your teen in the present. Get to know your teen. Do not confuse acceptance of him or her as a person with always agreeing with your teen's choices and behaviors. Likewise, allow your teen to get to know you as an authentic person, especially by spending time together—time apart from when you need to set limits or impose consequences. Also, be willing to admit your mistakes. This does not negate parental authority. Instead, admitting your mistakes expresses your courage to be authentic within the relationship.

Being authentic as a parent is not the same as being an open book. There are limitations to the types of interactions suitable for you to have as a parent. You need to be thoughtful in your level of self-disclosure, not because you want to deceive but because it might create difficulties in providing necessary limits and consequences. For example, be careful in sharing your own past drug use, if any, until you are sure your teen is mature enough to understand that sharing does not mean you are giving blanket permission to use. Remember that authenticity means being real, but not by sharing adult details of your life that are beyond your teen's level of maturity to process.

Finally, reinforcing your teen's ability to form meaningful relationships includes teaching them about trust. Trust is a necessary prerequisite for meaningful relationships, as the qualities of authenticity and reciprocity are based on trust. Strive to be trustworthy as a parent in keeping your word. Just as important, learn to impart trust to your teen. This can be difficult to do if trust has been broken in the past. But without granting your teen the opportunity to prove trustworthy, the relationship suffers. Lack of trust creates a barrier between the two of you, because it demonstrates a lack of faith in your teen. Opportunities to build trust should be measured, safe, and based upon past behavior. In other words, don't give carte blanche trust, especially in areas of past self-defeating or self-destructive behaviors. Start small, and then gradually expand these opportunities based on your teen's success in demonstrating trustworthiness.

Meaningful Relationships
Create a Willingness to Follow Healthy Structure

You already know that the first step in internalizing healthy structure involves learning to tolerate, through self-soothing, externally imposed behavioral expectations, limits, and consequences. Self-soothing is key to the process as toleration of external structure requires controlling impulses and handling strong emotions. Using the scene from the movie *The Break-Up* as the metaphor, your teen needs to be able first to tolerate doing dishes, despite having no desire to do so.

Meaningful relationships that promote cooperation and compromise allow your teen to take the next important step—that of wanting to do the dishes for the sake of someone else. The willingness to tolerate voluntarily acting counter to impulsive desires develops first within meaningful relationships. Gradually, these relationships have more influence on your teen than other types of relationships. The level of closeness, sincerity, cooperation, and respect that develops within these relationships creates a **willingness** in your teen to forgo impulsive and self-serving behaviors. This extends to becoming more willing to abide by the behavioral expectations of parents and other adults who display the qualities of meaningful relationships. In turn, your teen becomes more willing to follow voluntarily the behavioral expectations of others such as mentors and more advanced peers with which your teen has a meaningful relationship.

However, don't abandon all caution with regards to these relationships. Although positive mentors and peers who are able to form meaningful relationships with your teen likely also endorse healthy behavioral structure, you still need to know the perspectives and standards of those with whom you are encouraging your teen to form relationships. Proceed with safety in mind.

Let's take a look at a common real life example of how this willingness occurs with teens in academic settings. Consider a teen that begins to do much better in school. When asked why, the teen rarely points to the subject matter being of particular interest. Instead, the teen says, "I like the teacher." The teen may perceive no value in studying, but is willing to do so because of his or her relationship with the teacher. This willingness to act mature because of the relationship, even if the teen doesn't yet value such behavior, is the next step towards internalizing healthy structure in life.

Finally, promoting the development of meaningful relationships has benefits beyond just fostering your teen's willingness to tolerate acting mature. Meaningful relationships also provide opportunities to expand personal horizons. As your teen begins to want to behave differently for the sake of someone else, he or she also begins to become willing to try new things and to explore new perspectives for the sake of that person. If the other person values healthy pursuits, participating in these can positively expand your teen's life. It can open up his or her world to new adventures, perspectives, and interests in life that never would have been otherwise considered. Be it a new sport or even a new idea for a career, these experiences can be life changing.

Responding to Unhealthy Relationships

As in the case of the teen improving school performance, meaningful relationships tend to have a greater, more positive influence on the life of a teen than any other type of relationship. In fact, meaningful relationships can even outweigh the pull of negative peer pressure. However, these are not the only types of relationships that have a strong influence on teens. Intense, unhealthy relationships can affect the psychosocial development of teens—and not for the better. Because these relationships lack the important qualities that promote positive growth, they tend to undermine psychosocial development. If your teen is in an unhealthy relationship, providing opportunities for him or her to experience the qualities of meaningful relationships with you and others can be of great value. But parents also need to recognize unhealthy relationships and know how to respond.

In exploring several common types of unhealthy relationships, let's return to the example of Julie, the teen enmeshed in the relationship with her boyfriend. Her psychosocial development, especially in forming a healthy personal sense of self, is beginning to suffer. But what is enmeshment? Enmeshment is sometimes thought to occur when people become too close. This is a misnomer. Many relationships between people who are emotionally close to one another are quite healthy. Enmeshment occurs within close relationships when the personal boundaries that define each individual's unique perspectives, interests, emotions, and personal standards become overly blurred. In the process, authenticity is lost. Often, the relationship lacks a healthy balance of power as one member's interests and needs take precedence. In Julie's case, Bill's needs and interests outweigh hers. When one of the members in the relationship tends to be more self-absorbed, which is likely the case with Bill, the other individual tends to be more self-effacing and discounts his or her own personal needs, as Julie seems to have done.

Julie's efforts to cover for Bill's drinking may also be a sign that she is becoming codependent, a dynamic that can occur within enmeshed relationships. Codependency develops when one person begins to feel overly responsible for the other person's wellbeing, which can include cleaning up after poor behavior. Over time, the codependent behavior is perceived as part of the glue that holds the relationship together, but this requires the codependent person to sacrifice his or her own needs and personal boundaries to an unhealthy degree. Such is most likely the case with Julie. Keeping Bill happy, and sometimes rescuing him from poor choices, may have become a primary source of self-esteem for her as the codependent individual. If so she may begin to depend upon Bill's continued expression of need as his caretaker and rescuer. Julie may feel this dependency so strongly that unwittingly she may enable or support the continuation of Bill's negative behavior. The codependent individual sometimes will enable the negative behavior simply to remain in the role of caretaker and rescuer.

Do you recognize any of these dynamics forming in your teen's relationships? If so, you are not alone. Establishing personal boundaries is part of identity development. Confusing these boundaries within close relationships is common during adolescence. That's when enmeshment can result.

How can you respond in a manner that helps your teen grow beyond this tendency? The first step is by knowing how not to respond. You initial reaction may be to berate the other person or to forbid the relationship because the other person is somehow unfit. However, if personal boundaries are blurred, the resulting enmeshment creates the tendency to take anything negative said about this individual personally. Acting in this manner can actually strengthen your teen's resolve to remain in the relationship. Instead, consider focusing on behaviors rather than the other person's character. Set limits on any inappropriate behaviors occurring within the relationship, including any codependent behaviors. If the relationship is romantic, establish age-appropriate parameters for dating. Establishing limits and parameters requires them to choose whether or not to meet the behavioral requirements in order to remain involved. If one or both choose not to meet the behavior requirements, you have a much more effective tool than forbidding the relationship.

Please note one exception to forbidding a relationship. If the relationship is abusive, or if the relationship places your teen at significant risk of harm, then you as the parent have the obligation to require your teen to end the relationship.

If you see the dynamics of enmeshment, also seek to expand your teen's understanding of what constitutes meaningful relationships. Be a positive role model, and encourage your teen to be involved with other mentoring adults and positive peers. As your teen experiences these affirming qualities in others, gradually the tendency will be to seek to replicate these qualities within the enmeshed relationship. Conversely, your teen may begin realize the limitations and personal drawbacks of the relationship. If the relationship becomes so exclusive that it disallows these opportunities, consider placing a behavioral limit on the relationship that requires equal time be spent maintaining a relationship with you and other important individuals in his or her life.

If your teen is willing to talk objectively about the qualities that exist within the enmeshed relationship without feeling threatened encouraging this open discussion may achieve the same results. The goal is to help your teen move beyond enmeshment to prevent it becoming a long-term pattern of behavior within close relationships. If your teen won't open up either with you or another positive individual, consider counseling. The goal is for your teen to learn to recognize the dynamics of enmeshment and then to move beyond these dynamics in forming healthier relationships.

The example of Sophie demonstrates another situation where relationships lack certain key qualities that make them meaningful. In particular, what's missing are the important qualities of cooperation and compromise, or even a willingness to truly listen to one another. Instead, an ongoing rivalry exists where each friend strives to get her needs met regardless of the consequences to others, including friends. This aggressive competition is likely the result of Sophie's and her friends' collective struggles with self-soothing. Self-soothing struggles, combined with low self-esteem and a lack of experience with more meaningful peer relationships, results in Sophie and her friends clawing against each other. The self-centered antagonistic struggle between friends is in stark contrast to meaningful relationships, where each person mutually supports the other person.

If your teen seems to relate to friends in a manner similar to Sophie, a lack of self-soothing skills may be to blame. The lack of self-soothing skills results in meltdowns and the tendency to be self-absorbed in competitive, self-centered relationships. If your teen is like Sophie, consider ways to promote self-soothing in your teen. Strive to promote the development of more meaningful relationships, and consider counseling.

With existing friends, who are likely experiencing a similar developmental struggle with self-soothing, proceed with care. Prohibiting these relationships outright may reinforce your teen's resolve to remain friends. Instead, consider focusing on limiting immature behavior rather than prohibiting friendships. This needs to include limits on any inappropriate or unsafe behaviors that occur within these relationships. You may also forbid your teen to participate with these friends in certain social activities until they are able to act more mature. In most cases, prohibiting these friendships is not feasible anyway, as your teen will likely see these peers every day at school.

However, if associating with these peers places your teen at significant risk of harm or danger, make an exception. In this situation, you have to take steps to stop the interactions altogether whether by coordinating efforts with school officials and other parents or by removing your teen from the setting.

Let's move on to Mike. His scenario is another example of a teen that lacks meaningful relationships with peers. Mike's struggle is not just with a lack of certain qualities within relationships, but also with establishing peer connections in the first place. He desires peer friendships, but hasn't yet learned how to navigate the complicated social world of adolescence. Mike struggles because he lacks the necessary social skills. As a result, he may find it difficult to read body language and facial expressions. He may take things literally that are meant figuratively. He may misjudge the emotional states of others. Mike's lack of social skills results in him acting in ways that are socially inept or that may be inappropriate to the circumstances. Mike's social struggles may also be due to a Nonverbal Learning Disorder or Asperger's Syndrome (see *Appendix: Common Teen Disorders* for more information).

If your teen seems socially awkward, like Mike, be careful to avoid responding in anger or ridicule to any social faux pas. No doubt, your teen will be quite sensitive to his or her social shortfalls. Instead, empathize with your teen's sense of loneliness. Consider ways of promoting improved social skills. Seek to foster some social successes to serve as a base to build upon. Instead of treating your teen's social skills as soft skills learned through experience, consider them hard skills that require mastery through explicit instruction, similar to learning math or science. Through specific instruction, provided with patience and understanding, your teen's social skills will likely improve. There are social skill training curriculums available to assist in this process, and a therapist can also help facilitate social skill development.

In fostering social successes, encourage your teen to try out newfound social skills first with you and other adults that are accepting of your teen. Then, over time, with peers. With existing peers that perhaps have a negative opinion of your teen, the goal may initially be only to lessen your teen's distress by increasing his or her ability to form at least rudimentary social relationships with these peers. Eventually, perhaps these relationships can become friendships. Even if friendships don't evolve, any social success with these peers builds confidence and plants the seeds for further success.

Improved skills and increased success in social settings isn't enough. Your teen also needs meaningful relationships in life with folks with whom he or she can develop a real personal connection. With peers, search for opportunities for your teen to develop friendships in settings other than school, such as social groups or clubs focused on a particular shared interest. These interests can provide a social focal point within which relationships can form. The bonding that can develop in these settings can take some of the pressure off needing to be so socially adept.

Perhaps in spite of all your efforts, positive peer friendships remain sparse or are lacking altogether. If this is the case, don't despair. The point is not the age of the other person, but that a meaningful relationship exists. This means connections between your teen, you, and hopefully at least one other adult (which may be a therapist) can meet these needs. Remember: it is about the quality of the relationships, not the quantity of relationships. In addition, while peer friendships are great, adolescence doesn't last forever. The main goal is for your teen to learn to interact with adults, not other teens. This is why it is so important to promote your teen's ability to develop meaningful relationships with yourself and with other mentoring adults.

Meaningful Relationships: The Foundation of Identity Development

We've learned that nurturance and consistent attentiveness to a teen's needs by parents and other caretakers fosters self-soothing. The ability to self-soothe also promotes within teens the growing ability to tolerate, without meltdowns, externally imposed behavioral limits and the expectation to display mature behavior. In this chapter, we've seen how the formation of meaningful relationships develops when teens begin to consider the needs and perspectives of others in addition to their own. These relationships create such a level of closeness, cooperation, and reciprocity that teens begin to become willing to follow behavioral expectations to act more mature for the sake of the other person.

At this point, teens are more willing to act mature, especially when around those with whom they have a meaningful relationship. Yet something significant is still missing. They still have not yet internalized perspectives and behavioral standards of their own to any significant degree. This internalization of healthy structure begins as part of the process of identity development, another step in the upward spiral. Let's see how this next step works.

CHAPTER FOUR

INTERNALIZING HEALTHY STRUCTURE IN LIFE

Through others we become ourselves.

Lev S Vygotsky

Kelsey is an intelligent, energetic, sixteen-year-old girl who takes pride in her independence. She is quite particular in her choice of clothes, hairstyle, and makeup and adamantly disagrees with her parents when they suggest alternatives. She lets them know in no uncertain terms that she is her own person, and so shouldn't have to conform to her parents' wishes. Yet she seems unaware that her fashion choices and behaviors make her appear like a clone of her friends. When her parents point out the similarity, she gets upset and takes their comments as a personal insult. Why does Kelsey act this way?

We've seen how the importance of teens forming meaningful relationships encourages a willingness to change their behavior and act more mature for the sake of others. Acting more mature for the sake of relationships is an important developmental step in itself. But relationships also have a significant effect on the next stage of teen development—the active internalization of healthy structure in beginning to form an adult identity. Structure includes the perspectives used to evaluate if an experience is positive or negative and the parameters used to determine how to act towards oneself and others. Teens begin to internalize structure when they start to choose which qualities to incorporate in life through emulating the qualities they experience in their relationships with others. Meaningful relationships tend to have a greater, more positive influence on the life of a teen than any other type of relationship. Therefore, the goal is to promote the development of meaningful relationships with individuals that endorse healthy structure.

Because teens are still learning to develop meaningful relationships, often they are initially involved in less sophisticated peer relationships. Peer identification is frequently reinforced by the desire to be different from their parents in establishing a sense of autonomy, even when this means copying others. Consequently, until more meaningful relationships develop, often the relationships that initially have the most effect on teens are relatively immature peer relationships. This is what is happening with Kelsey. She is trying on many of the behaviors and perspectives of her peers in beginning to establish her identity.

If your teen is acting similar to Kelsey, it is helpful to understand how identity forms and that the behavior your teen is exhibiting is due to being in an early phase of identity development. Understanding identity development can prevent you from being confused by unexpected behaviors and help you better empathize with your teen's struggles with peer pressure and peer criticism. Understanding identity development can also reaffirm your resolve to foster meaningful relationships in your teen's life and can help guide your use of limits and consequences. In explaining identity development, let's begin by defining identity.

Identity Defined

Identity is the set of characteristics that define who a person is in relation to others. Characteristics include the qualities shared socially with others and the qualities that make each person unique. To understand identity, think of it as similar perhaps to an egg with three components. A protective outer shell comprised of personal boundaries. A second layer or social self that encompasses one's social identity and relationships with others. A central core or personal self that contains the qualities that make each person a distinct individual. Let's explore each, starting with the personal self.

Similar to an egg yolk, personal self lies at the core of identity. It is the last component to fully develop. Personal self is the collection of internal characteristics that a person uses to define him or herself. These characteristics provide the experience of being a unique individual over time and across social roles. Personal self is also the location of self-worth and personal morality. Although significantly affected by others, personal self is not a social experience, but a private recognition of one's own sense of self and individuality.

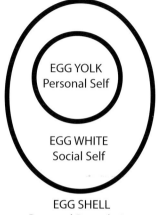

EGG YOLK
Personal Self

EGG WHITE
Social Self

EGG SHELL
Personal Boundaries

Surrounding personal self is the social self—the egg white. Social self, also sometimes called social identity, refers to the various personas and modes of behavior a person adapts in the roles played within relationships and society as a whole. Roles can be related to social functions, such as being a student, sibling, parent, friend, or employee. Roles can also be affected by sociocultural categories, such as race, age, or gender. Unlike personal self, which in a psychologically mature individual is experienced as more constant regardless of the circumstances, the qualities that comprise the social self are more fluid. They depend upon the setting and role one is playing at the time. For example, at work individuals take on a more formal business-like persona than with friends.

Similar to an eggshell one's identity is encapsulated by personal boundaries. Personal boundaries are the parameters that delineate one person from the next. Personal boundaries, at their most primitive, are the concrete characteristics that separate a person from the rest of the world, beginning with the recognition that one has a separate physical body. Physical boundaries, in fact, are the first boundaries that infants recognize in psychologically hatching, which is the process whereby infants discover that a separate world exists outside their own immediate experience. Prior to this recognition, infants feel no distinction between themselves and their primary caregivers.

Personal boundaries also extend to abstract characteristics, such as the perspectives and beliefs one uses to determine if a relationship is fitting and desirable. Personal boundaries also include specific behavioral standards or internal guidelines used to determine if certain actions are permissible. Altogether, personal boundaries represent the structure a person internalizes that serves as a template for understanding and interacting with the world.

Identity Development

How do these three aspects of identity develop? The process begins in infancy and early childhood. It begins as children first learn to structure their experience of the world and themselves, from the outside in. The first step is the development of primitive physical boundaries. Infants start to recognize that they differ from their primary caregivers. Gradually, they also recognize that many other objects are separate from them.

This recognition of separateness coincides with object permanence, the understanding that objects continue to exist even when they can't be immediately seen or heard. These objects are different from them and have recognizable traits that make up these differences. With parental assistance, children begin to organize objects based on these traits into concrete categories, such as people, trees, birds, and toys.

Recognizing that traits can be organized into categories is the beginning of the development of more complex physical boundaries. As their ability to categorize increases, these gradually extend to making distinctions within social relationships, such as distinguishing between parents, siblings, and friends. Categorizing people is the beginning of children's formation of more abstract social boundaries based on social role distinctions rather than simple physical differences. As they apply these physical and social boundaries to themselves, a rudimentary sense of social self begins to form.

As children's intellectual capacity to think increases with age, so does their ability to reason and to compare people and behaviors. As a result, the categories children use to understand the world expand to include such qualities as good versus bad and obedient versus disobedient. Because their experience is primarily with parents, children typically adopt their parents' definition of these qualities. Within important relationships, children also gradually begin to categorize themselves as either good or bad. This categorization of self is based upon how others respond to them.

At this point, children do not yet distinguish the qualities of social self separately from their experience of having a personal self. But rather than lacking a personal sense of self, the personal self remains primarily a direct reflection of social interactions and role expectations. Most children do not differentiate much between their personal and social self until adolescence—when they begin to individuate and form a distinct, self-directed sense of individuality.

During childhood, identity formation is primarily a passive process. The passiveness changes in adolescence as identity formation starts to become more active due to expanded abstract reasoning. During adolescence, teens begin to recognize that there are many possible choices and outcomes in any given situation. They can now actively choose which structure to adopt to guide how they think and act, instead of passively adopting primarily the perspectives and behaviors of their parents. In choosing to adopt a different structure, they assume a social self that is different from their childhood persona.

Given their drive for autonomy, this frequently results in an immature desire to be different from their parents, most often initially by copying peers. At this stage of development, even though identity development is a more active process, teens' cognitive development and personal experience is still somewhat limited. As a result, they do not yet discriminate much between the social identity that affiliations with peers provide and their personal sense of self.

Why is understanding identity development helpful to you as the parent of a teen? Simply recognizing that your teen has entered a new and crucial transitional phase in approaching adulthood can help. Your teen's attempt to copy peers is a normal part of identity development in beginning to differentiate who he or she is in relation to others. This differentiation usually begins with a level of separation from the people your child is closest to, namely you as parents. As a result, your teen is likely reexamining the perspectives, behavioral standards, and role expectations (or social self) he or she adopted from you as a child. This represents another cyclical turn on the upward developmental spiral.

Your teen now begins to deliberately choose whose perspectives and behavioral standards to incorporate in life—yours or someone else's. Your teen seeks differentiation, but the ability to do so primarily still only extends to choosing whom to emulate. Individuation requires the ability to selectively choose which qualities to incorporate in life and which ones to reject. Individuation requires further advances in abstract thought and social development. Your teen, therefore, initially knows no other way to begin to differentiate other than to be different from you by emulating others with whom he or she identifies. As paradoxical as it may seem, the first step towards individuation in your teen may very well be groupthink.

Groupthink and Development

Groupthink occurs when the members equate their personal boundaries with the perspectives and behavioral standards of the group and their sense of self with the group's social identity. For teens, guidelines they use to determine how to think and act are gained by adopting the values and behaviors of the group, and their overall sense of identity is dependent upon their social identity as part of the group. As such, groupthink is a sign of immature identity development. However, groupthink is not all bad. It is not considered pathological unless a teen identifies long-term with a particularly negative group or becomes stuck in groupthink indefinitely. As a transitional state, it actually represents an important advancement where teens now begin to choose, and hence to actively internalize, which perspectives and behavioral guidelines to incorporate in life.

Groupthink in teens during this early phase is quite powerful for two primary reasons. The first has to do with their level of cognitive development. An increase in abstract reasoning allows teens to recognize that there are multiple choices possible in most situations, but teens at this point still lack recognition of subtleties within these choices. Teens tend to perceive the world in all-or-nothing terms, where choosing to be like someone does not include the capacity for selecting certain traits. The result is either to identify completely with an individual or a group, or to avoid any identification at all.

The second factor that makes groupthink so powerful has to do with group dynamics. Groups tend to have collective norms and expectations that are enforced through pressure by other group members to conform. As a result, teens can find it difficult to go against these group norms. Group dynamics can also cause individuals to behave in ways that they normally wouldn't due to group pressure and to justify their actions by rationalizing that they were just going along with the group.

Teens' tendency towards all-or-nothing thinking combined with the pressure of group dynamics means teens often equate identifying with others as thinking and acting just like them. When the intensity of teens' identification with a group of peers deepens, their tendency to adopt unquestioningly the thoughts and actions of the group also increases. This identification can be so intense that teens may feel that they have no identity apart from their connection with the group. If your teen is in the midst of groupthink, you may see him or her strive to remain in constant contact with certain peers to the exclusion of others, spending hours texting or

on the phone. Teens can become frantic when out of touch. This tendency to be always in touch with peers is groupthink in action.

Until teens advance beyond groupthink, their personal self remains overly dependent upon adopting the actions and opinions of the group. Remember, their personal self is at the core of identity and controls their individuality. With their personal self still so dependent on the group, these teens do not yet think for themselves. In addition, this dependency on the group means that upholding the group's identity reinforces their own personal sense of identity. This dependency on the group for a sense of identity can reinforce the formation of both cliques and gangs.

Group Identity: Cliques and Gangs

Teen cliques and gangs are attractive because they offer a ready-made identity and an informal set of expectations to follow to be a member of the group. Expectations can include acting or dressing a certain way. The ability to meet the group's expectations affects who can be in the group, and who doesn't belong. For example, you can't be accepted as a jock if you're not athletic.

Let's look first at cliques. While the types and labels of cliques vary across different regions of the country, they usually include several common varieties. The following list is far from exhaustive, but provides a sample of some of the more common teen cliques. See if you can spot which clique your teen has begun to identify with or has difficult interactions with due to being left out.

- **Cool Kids:** Referred to as preps in some schools, this group is defined by their popularity and social standing in school.
- **Athletes:** Often referred to as jocks, this group is defined by their involvement in sports teams, a status that often confers a higher social standing.
- **Intellectuals:** Sometimes referred to as geeks or nerds, this group is defined by the members' academic prowess.
- **Social Activity Cliques:** These are groups defined by the ac-

tivities that members participate in together, such as cheerleading, band, choir, and drama.

- **Alternative Style Cliques:** These are groups defined by a style and interest that may be in sharp contrast with parents, such as goths, emos, or hipsters.
- **Alternative Activity Cliques:** These are groups defined by activities that skirt the edge of acceptability, like skaters or gamers. These are also groups that affiliate with drug use such as stoners or burnouts.

Your teen may also have experience with gangs. Similar in many ways to cliques, gangs also provide a ready-made identity, complete with expectations regarding how to think and act. Because of the ready-made identity they provide, gangs have a presence in high schools and within the larger adult community. Comparable to cliques, gangs also tend to adopt a certain style of behavior and appearance. However, gangs are more inclined to extend this focus to include certain colors or symbols that represent gang affiliation, in essence serving as a type of uniform.

The leadership in gangs is also usually more formal than the relatively informal leadership in most cliques. In addition, while gangs do in part exist because of the sense of identity they confer on individual members, gangs also exist for more nefarious purposes that include illegal activity. Due to illegal activity, gang affiliation is frequently taken much more seriously. As a result, attempting to leave the gang is met with greater resistance and sometimes retaliation, including physical harm or even death.

The sense of group identity that a clique or gang provides is reinforced not only by being a member, but also by the group's recognition of who doesn't belong. The group can distinguish those who don't belong because they don't measure up to the group's requirements. This measuring creates a feeling of group superiority over those outside the group. In turn, it reinforces the group's sense of pride and identity. Often, membership in certain groups occurs with a pecking order that provides teens more social status.

Teens who encounter the low end of a pecking order in social settings suffer an unpleasant and sometimes traumatic experience.

What is a pecking order? Pecking order refers to the status individuals or groups have within an established social setting, such as in a high school community. The phrase originates from a hierarchy that develops in chickens. To maintain dominance, birds higher in status physically peck those of lower status. Unfortunately, a similar process occurs within human communities. The members of a group higher in the pecking order tend to ignore at best and at worse vilify or pick on those lower in the pecking order. These negative displays of dominance reaffirm the persona of the group and by association the sense of identity of each member. This behavior also descends down the pecking order. Each group picked on subsequently picks on individuals or groups lower in the pecking order. If your teen has experienced being denigrated or ridiculed by members of another teen group, he or she is suffering under pecking order behavior. The group dynamics of pecking orders can undermine self-esteem and a positive sense of self.

Identity Confusion in Teens

Cliques and gangs are examples of groupthink's effect on an adolescent. Your teen has likely experienced and been impacted by at least some of these group dynamics personally. However, groupthink may also contribute to identity confusion in teens. Because teens often identify with multiple groups across various social settings, they can exhibit multiple expressions of group identity. This fluidity in expressing themselves is not problematic in and of itself. But if the personal self remains underdeveloped for too long, eventually teens begin to recognize a change in their overall sense of identity depending upon the group they are with. Their overall sense of identity can feel quite unstable. If your teen experiences this instability, these fluctuations can be quite confusing. Teens can feel unsure of their identity depending upon the group they are with at the moment.

The Identity Crisis of a Tomato

Tom often wondered on which side of the
crisper he really belonged?

Fluctuations in identity may cause teens to experience an existential crisis as they struggle to establish a consistent identity. Adolescents often reflect the struggle in music and poetry as feeling lost or that nobody really knows them. Too much struggle results in despair.

If channeled in the right direction, the struggle with fluctuating identities can become a positive dynamic in teens. It can allow teens to purposefully try on different identities. Like shoes, they can try on different sets of behavioral standards and perspectives to see what fits. The psychologist Erik Erikson calls this period of positive fluctuations during adolescence a developmental moratorium. A developmental moratorium is a socially acceptable delay that provides teens the opportunity to experience different aspects of identity before choosing which to ultimately incorporate in life.

In teens, identity confusion can also occur when the emerging personal self at the core of their identity cannot be reconciled with certain perspectives or behaviors of the groups with which they identify. For example, such a struggle can occur initially with lesbian, gay, bisexual, and transgender teens. Important aspects of their personal self may not fit with the boundaries and perspectives of the social groups with whom they belong—family, religious groups, or their cultural community. As a result, these teens can struggle with how to reconcile these differences. Until the struggle is resolved, it makes these teens feel different from others and can result in hiding or denying aspects of their personal self. Confusion and personal distress often result. Resolution comes through a number of factors. These teens must gain increased healthy individuation by defining their own personal self without being overly dependent upon other's perspectives. In addition they need to find acceptance within a network of friends and family, either by important groups becoming more accepting of these aspects of their personal self, or by finding groups more congruent with their emerging personal sense of self.

Information Technology and Groupthink

Information technology can intensify the effects of group-think. The explosion in information technology now allows teens to be in constant contact with peers and to interact with virtual groups all over the world as part of social media and on-line gaming. How is this technology a problem? For many teens, the use of digital communications, social media, and on-line gaming are just additional ways to do homework, recreate, and interact with peers. For these teens use is not problematic. But for other teens, the use of these technologies is far from harmless. See if you recognize any of the following behaviors occurring with your teen.

Our current technology allows teens to remain connected and plugged in twenty-four hours a day. Many teens even sleep with their cell phones, ready to respond to texts from friends at all hours of the night. This virtual umbilical cord can intensify group-think as teens are never apart from the group's influence. This can be problematic because these teens are never expected to think for themselves. In addition, with the expansion of social media, teens post and compare every aspect of daily life. Trying to prove who has a better life often forms a competitive undercurrent to these posts. Events of daily life become performances to be shared and evaluated by the group. Everything they do and think is evaluated through this competitive social filter. The social filter inhibits the formation of a healthy, individuated personal self.

On-line gaming has created virtual worlds. Within these worlds, teens establish a pseudo-identity in the form of a virtual self, or avatar. The virtual self interacts with others using behavioral standards that sometimes are quite different from what is acceptable in the real world. Many games even require a reversal of typical ethical standards in order to advance in the game. These games reward immoral and illegal behavior as part of the game's strategy. In turn, they encourage a moral inversion where what is considered bad or immoral in the real world is good in the game, and vice versa.

These virtual worlds can become very attractive. Teens never need to risk revealing or even developing a true personal self. They are so attractive, in fact, that some teens begin to identify with these virtual groups as their primary source of an emerging sense of identity. When teens primarily identify with a virtual source, they tend to cut themselves off from real relationships. Their on-line behavioral standards and persona, including any tendency to be aggressive or anti-social, spills over into the real world. For these teens, on-line groupthink begins to trump real life groupthink.

Dependency on the virtual world stunts psychosocial development. Virtual relationships are incapable of demonstrating the relational qualities necessary to promote healthy identity development. Because these virtual worlds are so attractive, reinforced by the fact that online games are purposely designed to foster compulsive play, prolonged use by these teens can also cause the development of a behavioral addiction (see *Appendix: Common Teen Disorders* for more information).

Promoting the Incorporation of Healthy Structure in Your Teen

Given the strength of groupthink, the potential for identity confusion, and the possible negative effects of technology, how can you promote the incorporation of healthy structure in your teen? You already know the first step—through promoting your teen's ability to form meaningful relationships and seeking opportunities for these to develop and expand. The depth and quality of meaningful relationships eventually outweighs the influence of other affiliations, including negative groupthink. Identifications that form within meaningful relationships occur at a much more substantial level. As your teen actively chooses how to think and act based on his or her identifications with others, if meaningful relationships exist, your teen is more inclined to internalize the traits of these individuals.

What behavioral traits is your teen likely to experience within these healthy relationships? At the very least, people who demonstrate the qualities of meaningful, healthy relationships are those that endorse authenticity, cooperation, reciprocity, empathy, compromise, and the desire to act in your teen's best interest. This is a pretty good start! Even so, as you review how to promote the development of meaningful relationships in your teen, consider who might be the best role model of healthy structure. Be aware that even those able to offer meaningful relationships to your teen may endorse significantly different perspectives and behavioral standards than yours.

Remember also that meaningful relationships should begin with you as a parent. Seek to exhibit the qualities that comprise meaningful relationships in your interactions with your teen. This will encourage your teen to consider choosing behavioral traits and perspectives similar to yours. It will also help him or her become more receptive to the intent behind the non-punitive limits and consequences you provide. Receptivity will reinforce your teen's internalization of self-limits on immature behavior and the rational thoughtfulness to consider potential consequences before choosing how to act. Examining and adjusting how you provide limits and consequences can further reinforce receptivity.

In reviewing how you set limits and consequences, ask yourself if the ones you provide are relationship-based. Limits and consequences need to be given with a spirit of relational understanding and support. To show this spirit requires maintaining perspective in order to display empathy when confronted with immature behavior, even when your teen is dismissive or angry with you. Seek to understand the circumstances surrounding immature behavior and consider how your teen's level of maturity may be contributing to the behavior. For example, instead of getting angry at immature behavior, recognize that the behavior may be a result of struggles with self-soothing or a lack of experience in remaining resilient in the face of peer pressure. This developmental perspective will temper your frustration. Maintaining developmental perspective also allows the type of empathic response that creates more openness in your teen to the lessons that thoughtful limits and consequences can teach.

But what about setting limits and consequences? Instead of just compliance, limits and consequences should focus on promoting the development of healthy internal structure. Developing such structure provides your teen a framework to consider options thoughtfully, and their potential ramifications, before choosing a course of action. This means focusing on consequences and not punishments. Let's examine the difference between the two.

Punishments are given in anger and involve actions usually intended to inflict emotional or physical pain. They are designed to accomplish two goals: to extinguish bad behavior and to impose retribution. Often given in anger by adults, they represent a form of revenge against being imposed upon, embarrassed, or defied. At best, this extinguishes negative behavior in the short run, but is proven to do little to promote long-term thoughtfulness in teens.

Consequences, on the other hand, are intentionally designed to promote thinking in teens by encouraging them to consider the potential effects of their choices. The goal is to promote reflection and deliberation in teens as they learn to make better choices in the future rather than to extinguish and punish current behavior.

In providing limits and consequences designed to promote thoughtful consideration and better decision-making in internalizing healthy structure, consider the following suggestions:

- Plan to provide limits and consequences throughout the entirety of your child's adolescence. While these need to be adjusted constantly to reflect the maturity level of your teen's behavior, don't assume that his or her increased autonomy means you can abandon this responsibility as a parent. Even older teens and young adults still need ongoing guidance in making choices and solving problems.
- Your expectations for your teen's behavior, and the limits and consequences you provide, need to be reasonable, age-appropriate, and rational. Unreasonable or unfairly applied limits and consequences will not promote thoughtfulness, but rather

confusion and anger.

- Your behavioral expectations, limits, and consequences should be predictable and consistent. Consistency sets the stage for rational consideration, especially when your teen is fully aware of the expectations and knows what to expect in choosing whether or not to follow them.

- Limits should include parameters on behaviors in areas that seem particularly problematic for your teen. Place behavioral limits on unhealthy relationships, substance abuse, and detrimental use of electronics.

- Consequences should be as immediate as possible. The further removed the consequences are from the behavior, the less likely your teen is to associate these consequences with that particular behavior.

- Consequences should be logical. Logical consequences reinforce thoughtful consideration because they match the specific situation both in form and in intensity. The best example of a logical consequence is allowing a natural consequence—such as letting your teen know that if he or she doesn't take care of a certain personal item, it will break. If your teen then chooses to be sloppy in taking care of the item and it does break, this is a natural consequence. Letting the teen live without replacing the item delivers natural consequences whereas immediately replacing the item rescues your teen. While not every situation lends itself to natural consequences, seek to duplicate this experience as much as possible. For example, for breaking curfew, consider consequences related to a loss of time, such as not being able to go out the following evening.

The Internalization of Healthy Structure: Incomplete Without Individuation

Providing reasonable, age-appropriate limits with predictable, logical consequences— combined with your efforts to reinforce the quality of your relationship with your teen— will help promote your teen's internalization of healthy structure. That internalization includes the inclination to be thoughtful in choosing how to act. Your teen's formation of meaningful relationships with individuals who also endorse healthy structure in life will also reinforce thoughtfulness in choosing how to act. The influence of these relationships eventually outweighs the potential negative influence of cliques and gangs.

However, as teens are still overly dependent upon the opinion and behaviors of others, internalization remains incomplete until teens develop a greater sense of individuation. Gaining that final step in identity development involves forming a personal self that is not so dependent upon an identity generated by all-or-nothing affiliation with others. Let's see how teens can gain the final step in identity.

CHAPTER FIVE

INDIVIDUATION: DEVELOPING A DIFFERENTIATED IDENTITY

To thine own self be true.

William Shakespeare

Christopher is seventeen years old. He does well academically and is usually pleasant and cooperative with his parents and teachers. But it hasn't always been so. Christopher went through a rough patch when he first entered high school. He seemed to drift away from his old friends and ultimately ended up associating with a negative bunch. His grades also dropped sharply. He became angry. He distanced himself from the family. Christopher's parents worried that his new friends were a bad influence and felt these relationships were contributing to his deteriorating behavior.

The summer between his junior and senior year Christopher's parents decided to make some changes. They shifted their schedule to make quality family time a priority. They encouraged Christopher to become involved in interesting extra-curricular activities led by positive adults and found a helpful therapist for him. Gradually, he began to interact more with his family and formed a good relationship with a teacher. Christopher also began to gravitate to a more levelheaded group of friends. Even his grades improved. All was not perfect, but the improvements encouraged his parents. They worried, however, what was going to happen when he went off to college in the fall, the next turn of the developmental spiral for Christopher. Could he sustain his newfound maturity, or would he once again struggle due to the influence of negative peers?

As the parent of a teen, perhaps you have similar concerns for your child. Even when he or she seems to be demonstrating more mature behavior, you may worry about how susceptible your teen remains to the influence of others. As you've already learned, this susceptibility is normal. The tendency to adopt the thoughts and behaviors of others represents an early phase of identity development. Teens develop their sense of identity first through their identification with others, which initially usually includes incorporating similar values and perspectives. During this phase of development, the major parental challenge is to encourage teens to identify with positive, impactful individuals. Through these meaningful relationships, teens try on and begin to internalize healthy structure as part of their personal boundaries.

When teens at this stage begin to identify with positive individuals, they do pretty well, but identity development doesn't end there. Teens can still be overly vulnerable to the influence of others. When placed in new situations with more negative people, they rapidly adopt the opinions and behaviors of this new group. At this stage, teens are unable to differentiate themselves, including how they feel and act, from the group they identify with at the time. Until they develop a distinct personal self at the core of their identity, they are incapable of consistently demonstrating stable boundaries and behaviors across different social settings. To stabilize boundaries and behaviors requires individuation, or the ability to distinguish a personal self that is separate from the identity of the group or groups with which they identify.

If your teen seems overly vulnerable to the influence of others, your teen also needs to begin to individuate. By developing an individuated personal self, your teen will be able to take more control in deciding how to act and what personal boundaries to uphold, even when experiencing peer pressure. Controlling behavior and boundaries allows your teen to begin to actively choose whom he or she wants to be, instead of passively following the crowd. In addition, healthy individuation supports further moral development, reinforces connections within the family, and sets the stage for further psychosocial development as a young adult. So what is required to take this next important step in psychosocial development? It may seem counterintuitive, but your teen's ability to establish a stable and mature personal self requires the ability to empathize with others.

Empathy and Psychosocial Development

The ability to empathize has a significant effect on psychosocial development, including individuation. Parents often overlook empathy assuming it to be just another social skill learned as part of growing up. This misperception is understandable as empathy does have a huge impact on social interactions and relationships. Teens with little empathy may have friends, but few meaningful relationships as their behavior towards others may be perceived as selfish and self-serving. Without empathy, teens can miss what another person perceives as important. For example, without empathy teens may not perceive that others are upset even in the face of tragedy, and may act in an insensitive manner.

But what is empathy? Empathy is a set of three related skills that include **emotional empathy, cognitive empathy,** and **social empathy.** The first two—emotional and cognitive empathy—directly affect the quality of a teen's relationships and the sense of connection the teen has with others.

Emotional empathy is often confused with sympathy. Sympathy involves acknowledging another person's distress, without necessarily understanding and sharing a similar emotional response. An example of sympathy might be acknowledging another person's loss without truly relating to the other person's feelings of grief. In contrast, emotional empathy is more than the recognition of another person's emotions. It requires being affected by the other person's emotions to the point of truly understanding what they are feeling. Developing emotional empathy creates connections within relationships because it allows a better understanding of the other person and their experience. Emotional empathy tends

"This is a real tragedy...
my reviews were a disaster!"

to reinforce relationships to a much greater degree than sympathy.

Cognitive empathy means being able to see the world from another person's point of view, to comprehend what it is like to be in their shoes. Rather than emotional receptivity, cognitive empathy requires developing the mental capacity to understand other people's perspective. Cognitive empathy supports the development of relationships because it allows teens to navigate complex social situations better by understanding the thinking behind other people's behavior.

Do you recognize emotional and cognitive empathy in your teen? As you consider the answer, recognize that teens display these skills inconsistently. Also, ask yourself: Do I display empathy consistently enough with my child? The question is important to consider because the ability to give and receive empathy is crucial to healthy psychosocial development. Empathic relationships provide your teen with the trusting secure base necessary to master self-soothing, and receiving empathy from others within relationships encourages your teen to express empathy in return. Empathic give-and-take reinforces meaningful relationships. But empathy's effect on psychosocial development doesn't end here. Empathy also affects your teen's ability to form a more autonomous personal self. Forming that self is made possible through the development of social empathy.

Social empathy is not really a third distinct type of empathy, but rather an expanded expression of cognitive and emotional empathy. Social empathy refers to developing the ability to empathize with others who are different from you. That ability requires an additional developmental step because empathizing with others that have a similar background and who share common values and experiences is much easier. Prior to the development of social empathy, teens often assume that important connections require sameness because they have never experienced a close relationship with someone much different from themselves. Social empathy is what allows your teen to begin to expand beyond these limits in forming relationships with people with different backgrounds and perspectives. Social empathy helps to dissolve the all-or-nothing belief that connecting and identifying with others requires being just like them. Cognitive advances that expand a teen's capacity to think more abstractly also reinforce the capacity for social empathy.

Relationships will likely expand with this new perspective. Expanded relationships bring the opportunity to experience new viewpoints and behaviors. Experiencing new relationships results in considering different options in life. More importantly, experiencing different options in life promotes the understanding that holding divergent viewpoints and valuing different behaviors does not conflict with having close relationships. Teens can then realize two important facts: that close relationships can exist with others that think and behave differently than them, and that they can, therefore, also choose to be different from others and still retain close relationships. This knowledge allows your teen to begin to selectively choose which traits to identify with in others, while choosing not to identify with all of these traits, without fear of losing these relationships. Developing social empathy allows your teen to choose thoughtfully the individual attributes that will comprise his or her own boundaries and personal self.

The newfound capacity to pick and choose which qualities to incorporate in life fosters the gradual development of an individuated personal self at the core of your teen's identity. Social empathy allows this individuation to occur especially through meaningful relationships that support differentiation. Becoming less reliant on mimicking others to have a sense of identity allows your teen to begin to the exhibit more mature and stable behavior based on an established, healthy personal self. In turn, a healthy personal self begins to reduce your teen's vulnerability to peer pressure from friends. Let's look at how the process works.

Social Empathy and Friends

While in the midst of groupthink, teens tend to adopt without question the majority of the traits and behaviors of their friends, both positive and negative, sometimes in spite of negative consequences. The adoption of these traits can be reinforced further by the tendency for teens to form cliques or gangs that actively reinforce the norms of a particular group. Adoption of groupthink is why your teen can be so vulnerable to peer pressure. For Christopher's parents, the potential reemergence of these dynamics creates worry. But social empathy begins to significantly change groupthink dynamics.

Developing social empathy allows your teen to form new relationships and to realize that thinking and acting just like existing friends should not be a requirement for being friends. In other words, social empathy leads to the recognition that true friendship should not require a person to give up who they are as an individual for the sake of the friendship. Realizing this distinction creates a more realistic view of existing friends, both their good and bad qualities. This insight also provides the opportunity to act based on a thoughtful personal evaluation of what is the best option, even when behaving differently than friends. For example, if your teen's friends put the pressure on to go to a party the night before a big test, this insight gives your teen the fortitude to stay home instead and study—without feeling like the decision undermines the friendship.

This change in perspective can be very freeing. When teens realize they don't need to cave into peer pressure to have a sense of identity, they can feel free to behave like themselves. When they recognize that peer pressure is not something a true friend should demand, the pressure turns off when faced with friends who act immaturely. Your teen can still care for these friends while choosing to think and behave quite differently. If friends accept the decision not to participate in the same behaviors, then the friendships usually continue. If instead these friends are intolerant of your teen's growing desire to be his or her own person, your teen likely will realize that they were not real friends in the first place.

"Your underwears not showing.
And where's your hat?"

Social Empathy and Principled Moral Development

Empathy, and in particular the development of social empathy, fosters an important advancement in adolescent moral development—from conventional to principled morality. You've already learned that conventional morality develops as your teen begins to care about others enough to behave differently for the sake of the relationship. That level of morality operates in contrast to pre-conventional morality where rewards and punishments are the only consideration. Similarly, a shift from conventional to principled morality occurs when your teen begins to develop social empathy.

Principled morality entails basing one's decisions on internalized ethical principles that extend across social situations. Principled morality emerges during the individuation process as your teen starts to actively choose what values to incorporate in life, instead of just going along with the behavior of the crowd. These personal values begin to become internalized as general ethical principles that make up a personal moral code. Your teen uses these principles as the moral foundation to help guide future decisions.

Researchers have identified two primary overarching principles that tend to form the basis of principled morality. These two lie on a continuum.

Towards one end of the continuum lies the principle of justice. Psychologist Lawrence Kohlberg, who discovered this principal by studying men, found that those he studied tended to base their morality on rules of justice delineating right from wrong. These are usually congruent with society, but sometimes may include personally held moral principles that conflict with conventional society. For example, the Tiananmen Square protesters of 1989 believed upholding democracy was a higher rule of justice than obeying an autocratic government.

At the other end of the continuum lies morality based on one's sense of ethical responsibility to care for others. Psychologist Carol Gilligan, who discovered this principle by studying women, found that those she studied tended to base their morality on what constitutes responsible, caring behavior towards others, even if at times it conflicts with societal norms. For example, Martin Luther King Jr. believed that it was moral to break unjust laws because they caused people to suffer.

As your teen develops a personal moral code, it will lie somewhere on this continuum. Actions will be judged based on principles of justice, or if the treatment of others displays ethical responsibility, or some combination of both. Although Kohlberg and Gilligan found indications that different genders seemed to gravitate towards different ends of the continuum, gaining more of a certain type of principled morality is not gender dependent nor is one end of the continuum necessarily better than the other. Wherever your teen falls on the continuum, principled morality develops when your teen decides what moral principles will underlie personal boundaries that guide future behavior. The development of a moral code is part of your teen's emerging personal self—a process that extends well into adulthood.

Social Empathy, Individuation, and Intimacy

Social empathy, and the establishment of an individuated personal self, also provides the foundation for the next step in a teen's psychosocial development as he or she becomes a young adult. Psychologist Erik Erickson described this step as learning to develop intimate relationships. Intimate relationships, according to Erickson, are not sexual relationships. Instead, intimate relationships are those that build upon the attributes of meaningful relationships (e.g. authenticity, cooperation, compromise, and reciprocity). They expand to include the experience of love, companionship, and personal commitment. In this way, all intimate relationships are meaningful, but not vice versa. For example, a relationship with a mentor, such as a teacher or coach, may be very meaningful, but not contain the intimacy of a relationship one has with a best friend or a romantic partner. Sexual behavior devoid of love and personal commitment lacks intimacy, as defined by Erickson.

As your teen becomes an adult, developing intimate relationships includes establishing life-long friendships that transcend common interests and experiences. Part of developing intimate relationships often includes forming a committed partner or spousal relationship too. Developing the capacity for intimacy is a long-term process that extends into the mid to late twenties and beyond. To develop intimacy at this level requires a willingness to accept the other person for whom he or she is and developing the personal fortitude to risk being authentic within the relationship. Both of these skills require social empathy or the ability to accept differences within relationships. Mature individuation in both members of the relationship is also necessary, which includes differentiating from one another without fear that the other person may abandon the relationship. Close, meaningful relationships that encourage each partner to retain their individuality bear the mark of intimacy.

Without the level of intimacy that healthy individuation fosters, relationships that develop in young adults will tend to be immature. In immature relationships, each member's personal self remains relatively underdeveloped. Within these relationships conflict or alienation is often the result, as each individual strives to gain an immature sense of self through the relationship. Disappointment and disillusionment follow, as inevitably neither lives up to the other person's expectations and demands. Immaturity can produce close, but very stormy and volatile relationships.

Alternatively, an inability to form intimate relationships can also lead to what Erik Erikson describes as isolation. Isolation includes a person that lacks relationships and individuals who have many relationships but still feel quite lonely. Isolation occurs when relationships lack the positive qualities of intimacy. Relationships may exist, but are sterile and lack the elements necessary to provide relational sustenance. These relationships result in emotional isolation and loneliness.

Individuation supports the ability to form intimate relationships. In turn, healthy intimate relationships also support positive individuation. Healthy intimate relationships foster a level of inter-dependency that reinforces within each member an individuated, personal self. These relationships provide support and encouragement to reach one's unique potential and a level of emotional companionship that only intimacy can provide. Being able to form relationships at this level is a key developmental task for teens as they mature into young adults.

Individuation and the Family

Healthy individuation in your teen also changes the dynamics within your family. Many teens initially believe that they must completely separate from their parents to be their own autonomous person. Due to the all-or-nothing misperception that to be close to and identify with someone requires being just like them, teens differentiate from their parents by looking and acting distinctly different from them. However, because teens continue to need the ongoing reassurance of a secure base in their lives, they only separate partially from their parents. That partial separation results in teens rapidly flip-flopping from seeking closeness with their parents especially during times of stress to denying their need for closeness especially when around peers. After all, peers have the same misperception, so they deem associating with parents as uncool. This is why you may have experienced your teen's efforts when around friends to avoid being seen with you!

Here's another example of how teens sometimes show their need for their parents: while desperately trying to deny this need, they constantly get into trouble or into situations where they require their parents' help. Overtly, these teens proclaim that they have no need for their parents, but still end up behaving in a manner that keeps their parents micromanaging their lives. Often these teens are unaware of what is occurring with their behavior. But whenever things go well enough that parents feel they can back off, these teens act in a manner that requires their parents to once again intervene. If this seems to be occurring in your family, often

"I thought it was sweet when Lisa gave me this bracelet, until we went to the mall and it shocked me every time I got within 30 feet of her and her friends."

a therapist with an awareness of family dynamics can help.

In whatever form the tendency for teens to distance themselves from their parents takes, this seemingly irrational behavior is reinforced until teens develop a healthy sense of individuation. If these dynamics are occurring in your family, they will continue until your teen develops social empathy. When teens develop social empathy, they recognize that not only can they choose to be different from peers without sacrificing friendships but concurrently can also choose to have similarities with their parents without sacrificing individuation. For your teen this means that his or her sense of individuality does not have to feel threatened by having things in common with you. Developing a healthy individuated sense of self can actually bring you and your teen closer together.

If your relationship has become distant, individuation sets the stage for an important reconnection—one where your teen will slowly become more open to receiving emotional support and advice from you. Once your teen realizes the pointlessness of rejecting your values just to be different from you, your teen may readopt many previously rejected family values. Often, these family values are the most congruent with the person your teen is choosing to become.

Promoting Healthy Individuation in Your Child

Promoting individuation means supporting your teen in learning to be a genuine individual with a healthy individuated personal self. To do so, you must allow differentiation in your teen by tolerating different perspectives from yours and by encouraging your teen to make more autonomous decisions that he or she appears mature enough to make safely. In simpler words, provide your teen a range of options within the limits you set and allow your teen to try his or her wings in age-appropriate situations. Remember: continue to be consistent with setting limits on immature behavior.

When your teen's behavior demonstrates positive forward momentum, do your best to support it. You'll need to support your teen's decisions when headed in the right direction, even if they are not what you would have chosen. If you are over-controlling, your teen won't learn how to problem solve and manage life. You may also inadvertently increase your teen's hesitancy to come to you for guidance. You may struggle in watching your teen develop different interests and perspectives from yours, but trying to force your teen to remain just like you may actually push them further away.

Work to reinforce the development of empathy in your teen. As you learned earlier, developing empathy is very important to healthy psychosocial development, including individuation. In promoting empathy development, remember that empathy is in large part learned through example. Therefore, strive to empathize emotionally with your teen. This includes empathizing with any distress experienced due to difficult circumstances or any anger related to limits you need to place on immature behavior. Strive to also understand your teen's perspectives or opinions, even when you don't agree. This demonstrates cognitive empathy. Striving to understand your teen's perceptions can be difficult to do when these perspectives seem skewed or overly immature, but role modeling cognitive empathy is critical. This role modeling requires separating how you respond to immature behavior when providing limits and consequences from how you respond to your teen as a person. Even when you need to impose limits due to immature behavior, show that you are willing to make the effort to understand your teen's point of view.

Beyond role modeling empathy, seek direct ways of expanding your teen's ability to understand the feelings and perceptions of others to further encourage the development of emotional and cognitive empathy. But where can you start? Try encouraging your teen to get in touch with his or her own emotions and perspectives in life. This self-empathy sets the stage for becoming more in tune with others. If we don't understand our own emotions and perspectives, we will struggle with understanding the emotions and perspectives of others.

Building upon this personal awareness, urge your teen similarly to identify the feelings and perspectives of others. To facilitate this identification with others, ask your teen to imagine what the other person is thinking or feeling in a particular circumstance. Then, if possible, suggest sharing his or her perception with the other person to verify the accuracy of the speculations. If your teen is open to it, this process can even include role-playing the other person's response to a specific circumstance. This process can be particularly effective if a conflict exists with the other person, as seeing the other person's point of view can lessen the intensity of the conflict. If you are concerned about your teen's level of empathy, group therapy can also be a great tool for learning how to grasp the emotions and perspective of others.

In supporting the development of emotional and cognitive empathy, you will likely find that your teen will first demonstrate these within relationships with others that share similar interests and traits. Demonstrating emotional and cognitive empathy with these individuals is an important early step forward, so employ positive recognition and reinforcement of these signs. As opportunities arise, consider ways of building upon these advancements by encouraging your teen to extend into empathizing and connecting with people with different interests, experiences, and opinions. Stretching your teen's scope increases the capacity to empathize in developing social empathy.

In setting the stage for social empathy to develop, consider reading books or viewing movies together that explore the perspectives and feelings of others in various situations and across different cultures. Afterwards, discuss these books and movies together with your teen. Allowing open sharing of thought can help expand your teen's perspectives.

Build upon this intellectual introduction to different perspectives by seeking opportunities for him or her to get to know others who have backgrounds and experiences that contrast from yours as a family. Consider taking a family vacation that introduces your teen to a different culture, or join a social group or volunteer experience that mixes people from different backgrounds and/or generations. You can also simply remain open to forming friendships and encouraging your teen to form friendships with people outside your typical group. Then, talk together about these experiences. Encourage your teen to consider the different perspectives and responses of these individuals.

Social empathy can also be encouraged by involvement in activities with adult mentors and positive peers beyond the family. This involvement stretches your teen's repertoire of experience, especially if these individuals challenge your teen to explore new interests and perspectives shared by others. A variety of settings can offer these challenges such as: taking music lessons, participating in sports, joining an organized group or after-school club, and even finding part-time employment where the supervisor is understanding of teens. Volunteering can also be a great experience. Often, it really helps teens see beyond their own viewpoints in learning to relate to others who are different from them. Volunteering can be a life-changing experience for teens.

As you see your teen start to exhibit social empathy toward others, consider ways of encouraging him or her to apply the same logic in developing an individuated personal self. When your teen begins to realize that connections are possible even with others with different perspectives and experiences, support the corresponding recognition that your teen can be different from others without sacrificing important connections. This recognition then encourages your teen to choose whom to become as an individual, without feeling the need to copy others.

To Thine Own Self Be True

We've looked at individuation—the process by which your teen develops an individuated personal self at the core of his or her identity. Individuating is what allows your teen the freedom to choose whom to become. But in remaining true to his or her personal self, the capacity to act on this newfound individuation may still be tenuous. The final step in strengthening individuation in your teen requires reinforcing resiliency. Let's look as ways to fortify resiliency.

CHAPTER SIX

BECOMING RESILIENT

I know you've heard it a thousand times before.
But it's true…if you want to be good,
you have to practice, practice, practice.

Ray Bradbury

During her freshman year in college, Amy seemed to be at a crisis point. It came as a shock to her parents as she had come so far from her earlier struggles. High school had been a challenge for Amy, especially finding a good group of friends. She had always felt shy and worried that she didn't measure up to the other kids. Eventually, Amy gravitated towards a negative group of peers. These friends liked to party hard and often used alcohol or marijuana even at school. She began to use with these friends, and followed their lead in sometimes skipping out of school. As a result, her grades began to drop. Her efforts to cover for her plummeting grades resulted in being caught cheating on multiple assignments.

In addition, Amy became more promiscuous especially when using. Even though she failed to feel enjoyment in promiscuity, it brought her more attention from boys. She felt good with these friends while partying, but often felt bad about herself afterwards. Despite her post-partying regret, she vehemently defended these friends to her parents and defied their requests to stop associating with them. When the school suspended her for drugs in her locker, her parents decided to make some changes.

Amy began to turn things around after the better part of a year of both individual and family counseling combined with efforts to expand her relationships to include more positive influences. Her parents paid extra attention to ensuring that the limits and consequences they gave were logical and delivered with empathy—including for the poor choices she sometimes made with friends.

The process seemed to make a difference. Amy's grades began to improve. While she still remained acquainted with many of her negative peers, she no longer felt the need to emulate their negative behaviors. Her circle of friends also expanded to include more positive, future-oriented peers. Amy even began to make plans to go to college. That spring, Amy's parents breathed a sigh of relief when she received her high school diploma.

College started off pretty well for Amy. Dorm life had its drama and conflicts with peers, but she seemed able to handle things well. With her midterm grades better than expected, she felt proud of how far she had come from her low point in high school.

Then came the day when her professor caught her cheating on a test. Rather than studying the night before, she had chosen to go to a party with some friends. Because her professor knew how hard she had worked in the class up to that point, he decided not to kick her out. But failure crashed down on Amy. To her, the event was a repeat of her high school failures all over again. She felt so ashamed. This one failure eclipsed all of her accomplishments. Calling her parents in tears, she begged to drop out of school. Upon their arrival on campus her parents could tell that she had been drinking. As they began to discuss the situation with Amy, they couldn't help but begin to wonder if perhaps she wasn't back to square one. Under the circumstances they had to ask themselves the painful question: Is our daughter really any more mature now than when she struggled so much in high school?

Amy is in the midst of a behavioral regression, something that all teens and young adults face to various degrees. Regressions occur. No surprise. Psychosocial development is not a linear progression, but a series of recurring cycles where skills are reworked over and over again throughout life. The goal is to strengthen these skills throughout the process producing cycles that form an upward spiral.

Even though regressions can eventually produce an upward spiral, this doesn't diminish how difficult these situations can be for both parents and teens. Regressions require a challenging re-working of previously learned psychosocial skills. A young adult's ability to face these situations determines how quickly and effectively he or she can work through these cycles when they occur. As these skills become stronger, regressions become less frequent and intense. When they do occur, they can also be of shorter duration. Knowing how to respond to regressions when they happen reinforces a teen's ability to work through regressions quickly and to learn from them. How can you reinforce your teen's ability to face effectively another turn in these developmental cycles when they occur? Through supporting resiliency in your teen.

Resiliency involves developing an increased ability to use one's psychosocial skills consistently in difficult circumstances. Resiliency includes reducing the frequency, intensity, and duration of regressive behaviors. It also entails knowing how to rebound from regressions when they occur.

How is resiliency developed? It requires practice in using one's psychosocial skills. Similar to physical endurance training, practice increases your teen's ability to use these skills for more extended periods of time and in more challenging circumstances. Your teen can also develop resiliency by practice in learning how to respond to regressions when they do occur. Regressions are inevitable, but they do not have to terminate a teen's upward developmental progress. If handled well, practice in the process of working through regressions actually boosts psychosocial maturity by increasing resiliency and further skill development.

Practice in Self-Soothing

The psychosocial skills you've learned about in this book build upon one another as a series of four stages. But don't be misled: four stages may seem to imply that once a skill is learned continuing to work on it is unnecessary. This is incorrect. Each of these skills needs constant attention and ongoing practice to build resiliency. These stages include the foundational skill of self-soothing.

To quickly review, self-soothing reduces impulsivity, meltdowns, and self-absorbed behavior. Reduction of these behaviors supports the capacity to delay gratification and sets the stage for meaningful relationships to develop. In turn, teens gain the foundation for the internalization of healthy structure. Because this process is cyclical, ongoing efforts to increase one's ability to self-soothe also promote each of these later skills. (If you need to review ways of fostering self-soothing in your teen, look back at Chapter Two.) But be wary of one of the more common roadblocks to practice in self-soothing— well-meaning parental interference. As both the author and a parent, I speak from personal experience: well-meaning interference has always been my tendency with my children. Practice in self-soothing requires allowing teens to go through periods of emotional pain and anxiety in learning to face difficult challenges and emotions.

Allowing your teen to face difficult emotions and to go through struggles can be tough as a parent. Often these are not recognized as opportunities to learn self-soothing, but instead as painful experiences from which to shield your teen. This is understandable. As parents we often feel that our job is to protect our child from anything difficult. Because we care so much, watching our child in emotional distress can hurt. However, it is important to recognize that unless the situation is too overwhelming or traumatic, rescuing your teen from emotionally demanding circumstances eliminates their opportunity to practice self-soothing. This reduces resiliency, which can be especially problematic when your teen becomes a young adult.

The tendency to rescue your now older child from emotional distress is fueled primarily by the closeness you share. This closeness often initially includes a level of shared boundaries, which involves empathizing with your teen and feeling his or her pain as if it were your own. Until adolescence, this tendency to treat you child's pain and struggles as your own is not a problem. In fact, it may have initially been useful in assuring that your child received the parental attention required when he or she was younger. Now that your child is a teen, this lack of differentiating your child's struggles from your own increases rescuing behavior that, in turn, reduces your teen's opportunities to practice self-soothing and problem-solving skills.

The tendency to rescue can also be combined with a tendency to take your teen's poor behavior personally. Without the necessary level of differentiation, you may end up interpreting things your teen does as a reflection on you. This misperception may result in believing that you are responsible to fix your teen, and that their struggles are your fault. Feeling at fault for your teen's struggles can reinforce the tendency to rescue out of a sense of guilt that you are somehow to blame for your child's struggles.

Another common response is to be over-controlling and to rigidly demand certain behavior to force your teen to become more mature. Over-control and rigidity is usually combined with intense anger and harsh punishments when your teen doesn't meet your demands, instead of emotional empathy and logical consequences. As you've already learned in Chapter Two, practice in self-soothing requires a secure base, fostered in large part by emotional empathy. Being angry and over-controlling undermines this secure base, which actually increases strong emotions and resistance.

The tendency to be either too soft by rescuing your teen or too demanding and punitive comes from a lack of objectivity. Promoting maturity means allowing your teen to begin to separate appropriately from you. It also means you need to begin to separate from your teen. This separation, or differentiation, provides the objectivity necessary to allow your teen to practice self-soothing without being too quick to rescue, and to support self-soothing through empathy instead of taking your teen's immature behavior personally. As a parent, how can you separate emotionally from your teen in becoming more objective? Through applying social empathy in a manner remarkably similar to how social empathy allows your teen to begin to differentiate from others.

Applying social empathy involves recognizing that the connection you share needs to be balanced with the realization that your teen is a different person than you. The parent-child relationship does not equate with treating your child as an extension of yourself. You are there to provide support and to increasingly allow your teen to learn how to handle difficult situations and emotions more autonomously. These tough emotions need to be treated as your teen's emotions, rather than yours to take away. Immature behaviors and mistakes are also your teen's to face. They are not yours to own and attempt to control. Realizing your differences allows objectivity in deciding how to respond to your teen, without feeling that you are rejecting the closeness you share. Objectivity reduces the likelihood of overreacting either by rescuing or by becoming so upset that instead of promoting self-soothing you stir up distressing emotions and further resistance in your teen.

Developing the level of objectivity described above may seem like an abdication of your love and concern as a parent. But the objectivity that social empathy provides is actually intended to be a more advanced expression of your love and concern. It makes you better equipped to act in your teen's best interest, including promoting practice in self-soothing and problem solving. Don't equate your own increasingly objective and even-keeled emotional responses as in any way negating your relationship. As a good parent, you are gradually handing over responsibility for your teen's life to him or her.

But don't assume that increased objectivity means never stepping in to help. There will still be times when you must intervene in your teen's best interest. Intervention is required especially if circumstances are unusually harsh, traumatic, physically or emotionally dangerous, or beyond your teen's ability to emotionally manage. While learning how to self-soothe and face trying circumstances is important, during the process situations may arise that your teen isn't yet mature enough to handle. It is best if your teen is able to practice more autonomy in handling tough situations when

"He's just a little dragon,
but let me know if you need any help."

you are still there to help if they get into situations they are not yet prepared to successfully manage.

Relational Practice

I've said much in this book about the importance of relationships, including the need to foster relational skills in your teen. Relationships are key to psychosocial development. In Chapter Three, you learned the qualities of meaningful relationships. I also emphasized how your relationship together remains your teen's secure base and is the primary source for learning and practicing how to form meaningful relationships. Your relationship is the initial template your teen relies upon in learning how to relate to others. Because teens learn about relationships from you, parenting can't be only about providing limits and consequences. The quality of your relationship with your teen is very important too.

How do you invest in the relationship especially if your teen seems emotionally nonresponsive? I am reminded of a story a parent once told me about his daughter who had become quite moody and isolative. The father was at a loss, but still sought to retain his connection with his daughter. At least once a day, he found the opportunity to kiss her forehead and to tell her he loved her. His actions seemed to fall on deaf ears. But gradually she seemed to rejoin the family. In the process, this act became an important family ritual for her. She even sought out a kiss on the forehead at times when he forgot. As she became a young adult, she was able to share how much that meant to her. Although her father had felt at times like he kissed a prickly cactus, his message got through that he cared for her and that their relationship was something important to him. His investment of time and energy was well worth it, even if at the time it didn't seem to have any effect.

Practice with Healthy Structure

Psychologist Viktor Frankl is quoted as saying: "Between

stimulus and response there is a space. In that space is our power to choose our response. In our response lies our growth and our freedom." It is the freedom to actively choose a response, instead of just passively reacting to short-term impulses, that allows teens to make better decisions as they enter adulthood. The freedom to choose requires the ability to self-soothe in order to utilize the space between stimulus and response in considering one's options before deciding upon a course of action.

How one utilizes this space is dependent upon one's level of internal structure. Mature internal structure is the ability to rationally consider consequences and to choose a positive course of action. Practice in external structure designed to encourage your teen to think through options, and to consider the consequences of their behavior, reinforces this level of internal rational consideration. Gradually expecting your teen to accept more responsibility for self-care, with you as a safety net, reinforces choosing safe, healthy options both now and in the future. Role modeling positive choices by individuals with whom your teen has a meaningful relationship encourages practice in trying out thoughtful decision-making. Consistent age appropriate limits and logical consequences support learning to make better decisions. Each example demonstrates how practice with healthy external structure strengthens healthy internal structure in your teen in learning how to productively use the space between stimulus and response.

Practice with Empathy

Your teen's ability to empathize will vary, especially when stress causes him or her to regress. In those moments, do your best to avoid becoming discouraged. Remember that adolescents are still learning empathy, and the sections of their brains related to empathy are still developing. Regressions related to displays of empathy are to be expected in teens.

Practice can reduce this tendency. Therefore, seek to display empathy routinely to your teen, and encourage your teen to practice considering what other people must be thinking or feeling in various situations. Also, seek opportunities to introduce him or her to folks with different experiences and perspectives in expanding practice in social empathy.

Practice in Being a Leader and/or Role Model

Identity formation and individuation involves learning to remain true to one's values, even in situations where others do not endorse them. Good practice for your teen in developing this type of resiliency is within his or her daily interactions with others. One especially good opportunity for practice is as a leader or role model. To be an effective leader or role model requires your teen to remain true to a set of standards and behaviors related to the activity or setting, be it scouts, clubs, church or synagogue youth groups, sports teams, being a volunteer, or even being a role model for younger siblings. These opportunities offer great practice in reinforcing resiliency, as a good leader or role model needs to uphold standards even when certain members of the group try to coax him or her to abandon them. Over time, this experience reinforces the strength to uphold the values necessary within the leadership role. This practice can then generalize to also help your teen learn to uphold personal values under peer pressure.

Practice in Handling Entitlement

Another area of practice for teens to develop resiliency is learning to handle entitlement. Entitlement can cause a regression in all areas from self-soothing to mature identity development. Entitlement occurs when teens feel owed material goods and adult autonomy beyond what is age appropriate and without having to make the necessary effort. Teens may believe that mature behavior should not be a requirement for getting what they want. Entitlement is a very self-centered attitude.

If you see entitlement in your teen, it may be linked to regres-

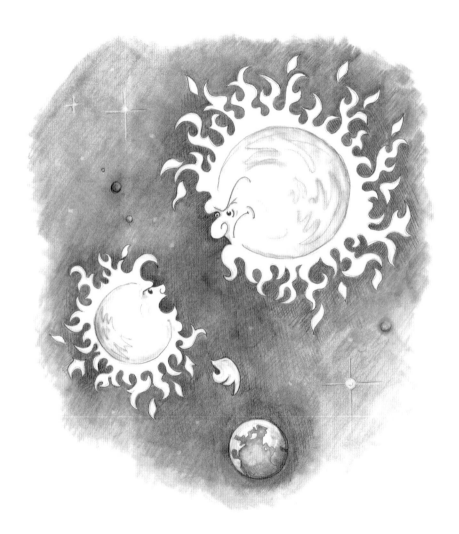

"DAD! THE WORLD DOES
REVOLVE AROUND ME!"

sive behavior related to self-soothing, which reinforces the tendency to be self-absorbed. Another reason you may see entitlement in your teen may be due to his or her vacillating level of empathy towards others. Without empathy, the focus tends to be primarily on oneself. Self-soothing and empathy are skills that, when practiced, can reduce entitlement. But the initial process of adolescent differentiation can also sometimes result in an increase in entitlement. Feelings of entitlement can arise when the self-worth teens begin to experience in becoming more autonomous becomes exaggerated through all-or-nothing thinking. Teens can then think that their worth is greater than others. When this occurs, teens assume that others should recognize their worth through catering first and foremost to their desires.

If your teen appears to have advanced in maturity, seems to be able to self-soothe and display empathy, but still begins to show entitlement, this is likely due to the early stages of differentiation. The entitlement you see may be your teen's immature attempt to seek external validation of his or her emerging sense of self-worth. Because entitlement seems to make your teen feel better, you may be tempted to give in and offer whatever is requested. However, any personal validation received through over indulgence can weaken your teen's resiliency as it undermines self-soothing, weakens his or her ability to manage discomfort, and reinforces a fragile sense of identity based on external trappings.

Because entitlement can be tied to your teen's emerging sense of identity and self-worth, responding to entitlement requires placing limits on indulgences while supporting your teen's self-worth. Teens need to recognize that self-worth is not dependent upon others giving them everything they want. It is about who they are as a person. In setting limits related to entitlement, remember to empathize with any distress and to reinforce your teen's worth as a person. Your teen may not be receptive to this support in the moment. But when the opportunity arises, reinforce that worth is based on internal traits, not on whether certain desires or demands are met. The more consistently entitlement is met through a combination of limits and positive affirmations, the less likely entitlement is to become a long-term pattern for your teen.

Practice in Rebounding from Regression

No matter how well developed the skills are, mistakes and regressive behaviors can't always be avoided. In fact, they are a part of the cyclical process of psychosocial development. Remember Amy and her parents? They were experiencing a regression. But while regressions are often disturbing, learning how to rebound from regressions can minimize destructive long-term patterns of immature behavior. Learning to rebound can further strengthen a teen's resiliency the next time he or she faces a similar situation, reinforcing the continuation of an upward developmental spiral.

Similarly to Amy, your child will also face regressions. What is important in these situations is to avoid dwelling on the negative aspects of the regression, but to reinforce learning how to bounce back. Learning to rebound from regressions is one of the most important things your teen can learn in becoming a resilient young adult! The only way to learn how to rebound from regressions is through multiple opportunities to practice. By supporting practice in working through regressions, your teen increasingly will become able to rebound independently. You can support rebound practice by focusing on three components: preplanning before a regression, recognizing the transient nature of regressions, and reinforcing each maturity skill in responding to a regression.

Preplanning before a regression involves pre-planning on two levels. First, preplanning begins with the framework for everyday life such as academic expectations, behavioral expectations, and what the consequences will be for potential foreseeable behavioral lapses. By having pre-established expectations created whenever possible with your teen's involvement, regressions can be addressed more effectively when they occur. Second, by preplanning your response can be more immediate, more understandable, and focused primarily on helping your teen thoughtfully decide what to do to get back on track. By having previously thought through together the likely outcomes of different foreseeable scenarios, any necessary consequences are also less likely to be perceived as arbitrary and punitive. Instead, consequences are more apt to be accepted as logical reactions to poor choices.

Preplanning before a regression also involves planning for the future. Future planning includes setting academic, vocational, and other goals, and working with your teen to make plans for achieving these goals. Cooperative preplanning helps provide a roadmap for the future. Long-term goals are sources of motivation that tend to reduce the frequency of regressions and compel your teen get back on track in life when setbacks do occur. Practice in learning how to plan for the future is also important. Learning to plan for the future is a vital skill necessary to face new, more significant challenges in life that require adjustments to existing plans.

Recognizing the transient nature of regressions means acting upon the understanding that regressions are temporary lapses into less mature thinking and behaving. Recognizing regressions as transient allows the realization that previously developed psychosocial skills are not lost. Instead, recognize that your teen is struggling to use these skills effectively or has chosen to avoid using them in a particularly challenging or stimulating situation. Regressive setbacks are part of a normal learning curve and represent one more turn in the spiral of psychosocial development.

The goal is to help your teen work through regressions by re-engaging and strengthening the psychosocial skills he or she already has and by learning new related skills. In this way, regressions, although painful and sometimes destructive, can also be great opportunities to encourage continued advancement in your teen's upward spiral in psychosocial development.

Given the pain and disappointment that often accompanies regressions, it is understandable that parents may worry that these setbacks are an indication that their teen has spiraled downward and is back to square one. But this perspective can make regressions longer and more intense. When your teen experiences a re-

Regressions may feel like your
teen went over a cliff...

... but the learning curve they provide
can propel your teen upward.

gression, do your best to avoid labeling the situation disparagingly as a return to square one. Labeling it negatively may extend the regression. Negative labeling of the regression can reinforce all-or-nothing thinking in your teen, which can cause your teen to lose motivation because he or she believes it means starting all over.

Reinforce each maturity skill in turn, beginning with the ability to self-soothe. Regressions can be related, at least in part, to your teen's self-soothing skills being overwhelmed. When this happens the result can be a meltdown or immature, self-absorbed behavior. During a regression, self-soothing skills may be tested even further if teens feel any guilt or shame because of their behavior. If this is occurring you may see one of two alternatives: despair with the message "I messed up and let others down so why try" or denial with the message "I didn't really care anyway."

During a regression, consider ways of supporting your teen's ability to self-soothe and reinforce his or her secure base. Provide this support by empathizing with the emotional struggles your teen experiences related to the regression, including any reactions to logical consequences that you need to impart. In reinforcing self-soothing, consider the following suggestions:

- Give the message that you know it must be difficult for your teen. Show genuine cognitive and emotional empathy to reaffirm emotional anchoring and that your teen can count on you and trust you to be there for him or her.
- Don't get mad. Don't lecture. Don't be sarcastic.
- Don't own your teen's struggles or blame yourself.
- Don't rescue your teen from facing difficult emotions and situations that he or she is capable of handling. Doing so limits opportunities to practice self-soothing.

Next, reinforce the ability to form meaningful relationships. During a regression, often your relationship with your teen is tested, and your teen may temporarily lose a sense of connection with you. Therefore, reinforce your relationship by reaffirming that you have faith in your teen. The realization that your relationship remains strong encourages your teen to be more willing to face difficult situations and emotions because of the relationship. Remember that under stress, including during a regression, your teen may become temporarily more self-absorbed which can stress your relationship. In reinforcing the ability to form and maintain meaningful relationships, consider the following suggestions:

- Give the message that you care about and have faith in your teen. Show that you haven't stopped caring because he or she is overwhelmed at the moment and is experiencing a regression.
- Continue to make the effort to reaffirm your relationship at times other than when dealing with a regression. Show that your relationship is based on more than responding to immature behavior.

Reinforce the ability to begin to internalize healthy structure. During times of regression, especially if it involves immature behavior, seek to help your teen reconnect with the mature structure he or she has previously been able to follow. Regressions may result in self-doubts. You want your teen to feel capable of choosing to adjust immature behavior in the present and to act more mature in the future. Assert your confidence in your teen's capacity to deal with the consequences, to act mature, and to choose to move in an upward direction in life. For example, in responding to their daughter's regression Amy's parents need to reaffirm for her how well she was doing in college up to that point and that they know she can continue to do well in the future. Similarly in reinforcing your teen's ability to live by internalized healthy structure, consider the following suggestions:

- Recognize past successes in adhering to healthy structure by giving the message that your teen has shown the ability to act mature in the past, including to correct mistakes. Convey you know he or she can do it again.

- Provide guidance and logical consequences designed to promote thoughtfulness in considering options rather than punishments meant to settle a score.
- When possible, give choices regarding the consequences experienced due to a regression.
- Don't rescue your teen from having to deal with the consequences of immature behavior. Being overprotective through rescuing gives your teen the discouraging message that you think he or she is incapable of handling the situation.

Finally reinforce your teen's individuation, or the growing ability to develop a differentiated identity. Along with encouraging your teen to choose to act mature, strive to support your teen in taking the lead in deciding what actions to take. This includes even when the choice isn't exactly what you would choose, as long as it is generally headed in the right direction. Supporting your teen in making the choice encourages ownership of personal values and perspectives in developing a core sense of self. It encourages your teen to think in developing solutions on his or her own. Through the development of a strong, positive, personal self, regressions become fewer and less intense. In reinforcing individuation in your teen, consider the following suggestions:

- Give your teen the message that you are there to help. But ask "What do you think you need to do to correct this situation?"
- Empower your teen to help decide upon reasonable consequences and/or restitution for immature behavior. If their ideas are unreasonable, you can still give them several choices to consider.
- Beyond consequences, empower them to help decide what to do next in getting back on track in life. Empowering them with the next step focuses the process beyond the regressive behaviors to deciding upon new and positive behaviors in the future.

By reinforcing each of these maturity skills, you assist your teen in reengaging and building upon these skills during and after a regression. The goal is to encourage them to think through their behavior in rebounding from a regression. A typical response may, therefore, sound something like this: **"I know this is hard for you. But I have great faith in you. I know you can do this. Remember when you handled something similar in the past? So what are you going to do to handle this situation, and how can I help?"**

It's Also About You as a Parent

In this book I've also given you suggestions for promoting psychosocial skill development in your teen. I've also given you suggestions for how you can respond as a parent to help reinforce resiliency in your teen. Practice in developing resiliency, including learning to respond successfully to a regression, reinforces future success in your teen as part of his or her upward spiral. But the spiral of psychosocial development doesn't end in adolescence. It applies to all of us throughout our life span. Let's move on to look at your own personal journey as an adult and as a parent.

CHAPTER SEVEN

THE SPIRAL CONTINUES

Growth is a spiral process,
doubling back on itself, reassessing and regrouping.

Julia Margaret Cameron

Today, my older daughter is a strong, independent and compassionate young woman, but her teen years were a bit of a challenge. She tended to act emotionally instead of rationally. Her relationships seemed strained. She often appeared scattered and doubted herself. She just didn't seem like the self-assured daughter I used to know. Since I am a big science fiction fan, the old 1956 movie *Invasion of the Body Snatchers* immediately came to mind. In the movie, alien duplicates emerge from huge seedpods to replace people. These duplicates are physically identical to the originals, but can be distinguished by certain alien traits and behaviors. Looking back, perhaps that movie was a peculiar association for me to make, but that is what it felt like. In many ways, my daughter seemed to be the same person, but her behavior and moods were different enough that I was tempted to check her closet for an empty seedpod!

But in addition to my daughter's behavior seeming a bit alien, my behavior seemed alien too! Becoming a teenager shook up my daughter's world, and the process shook up my wife's and mine as well. We found that our predictable life now took unexpected turns, and that emotional drama in the family seemed unavoidable. Providing limits was increasingly complicated, and we had to work to provide logical consequences. Over time, the stress affected my mood and even my ability to sleep. I also wasn't as sensitive as I

"Sure, all teens seem a bit alien...
but the extra legs are a real plus in soccer!"

used to be with my family. I sometimes found myself distracted and scattered at work. As a therapist, I knew what I was experiencing was typical. Nevertheless, I began to question my competency as a parent. I knew I was doing my best under the circumstances, but felt inadequate as I wasn't always the logical, nurturing, confident, and emotionally in-control father I wanted to be.

As a parent, maybe your experience is a bit like mine. Perhaps you too are sometimes at a loss regarding how to handle the chaos and anxiety that comes from having a teen in the house. Perhaps your teen's process affects your mood and behavior. Hopefully, I've helped by giving you a few ideas regarding how better to respond to your teen, but I would be remiss without also addressing your experience as a parent.

Why Focus on Me?

I realize that your motivation for reading this book most likely wasn't about exploring your own life, but to gain parenting ideas. However, to parent your teen effectively means you also need to focus on yourself. Why? As I've already pointed out, you remain pivotal to your teen's development. You are the primary source of your teen's secure base and are a key, ongoing provider of support, parental counsel, age-appropriate limits, and logical consequences. How you respond to your teen makes a big difference! Because of your importance to your teen's growth, ask yourself the following questions:

- Are there times when you demonstrate less than exemplary behavior as a parent? For example, when your teen acts immature, do you always retain the emotional fortitude to empathize with your teen?
- Can you consistently maintain perspective in these circumstances in order to thoughtfully choose how to respond?
- In addition, when your teen is in emotional distress, are you regularly able to remain objective, or are you too quick to res-

cue?

If you can't always answer yes to these questions, don't despair. Struggling, as a parent, goes with the territory of having a teen, which requires a reworking of your own coping mechanisms and psychological abilities.

I've described the development of psychosocial skills in adolescents as occurring in a cyclical fashion, with more advanced skills building upon previous childhood skills. All the changes teens face prompts this process, as childhood skills prove inadequate to meet all the challenges of adolescence. The task for parents is to help teens revisit and build upon these earlier skills in becoming stronger and more resilient. The effective reworking of earlier skills forms an upward developmental spiral as teens mature emotionally, socially, and psychologically in becoming young adults. But this upward turning of the spiral doesn't end with adolescence; it continues throughout life.

Any major change or stressor in life triggers a reworking of the same psychosocial skills first developed in childhood and subsequently strengthened in adolescence. Having a teenage child, although wonderful in so many ways, brings with it significant changes and stressors for you as a parent. As a result, just as becoming a teenager is triggering a reworking of previous psychosocial skills in your child, having a teenager triggers a similar process in you as a parent. Any struggles you may be having in responding effectively to your teen with both empathy and objectivity are likely related to this reworking. So let's briefly revisit the developmental spiral, only this time from the perspective of being the parent of a teen.

Adolescence: A Time of Change for Parents Too!

Your teen is not the only person facing a lot of changes in life. So are you as a parent. To begin, you have a child who is behaving in new challenging ways, perhaps pushing the limits of your family rules and your patience. As a result, you are faced with new

"I know the lyrics that
go with that ringtone young man!"

parenting challenges, including setting limits and providing logical consequences. Just trying to keep track of where to set limits in your teen's life has become increasing complicated!

In addition to the stress of attempting to maintain appropriate limits and consequences, having a teen may also stir strong emotions in you. You may feel anxious as worries for your teen's well-being increase, including concerns for his or her physical safety, emotional stability, and social adjustment. You may feel emotional pain seeing your teen struggle and allowing your teen to work through situations more and more on his or her own. You may also experience anger and resentment towards your teen when he or she defies you. That defiance may feel like a betrayal of your relationship. The combination of stresses can erode your emotional resilience and make it difficult for you to maintain the objectivity necessary as the parent of a teen.

Adding to this emotional stress, having a teen also signals the commencement of a new stage in life for you as a parent—that of an impending empty nest. Anticipating the imminent loss of your child's physical presence and reliance on you can cause feelings of depression or sadness. It can also make you reexamine your own sense of self due to significant changes in your role as a parent. Reworking your own psychosocial skills helps you learn to deal effectively with impending changes in your household and your role in it. Reworking your own psychosocial skills can make you a stronger person and help you avoid several common overreactions. These can include attempting to delay the separation by being excessively overprotective and preventing your teen from developing more autonomy, or by attempting to avoid prolonging the pain of separation by pushing your teen too quickly into adulthood. While both of these responses are common, neither is based on an objective analysis of what your teen really needs from you.

Beyond the specifics of adjusting to the changes in your teen's life, there may be other changes in your life occurring at the same time that are adding to the need to rework previous skills. Things like changing jobs, marital conflict, remarriage, physical illness, or experiencing a significant loss can add to the need to rework your skills. For any adult, these situations can emotionally overshadow one's life. Facing any of these situations can compound the difficulty you experience in responding to your teen in an objective manner. To do so requires first revisiting your ability to self-soothe.

Revisiting Your Ability to Self-Soothe

Self-soothing with a teen in the house can be quite a challenge. No matter how much you love your teen, parenting a teen can be quite exasperating due to the changes a teen brings to your life including his or her tendency to respond emotionally instead of rationally. As we saw back in Chapter One, until your teen's prefrontal cortex is fully developed, he or she will tend to respond first from the limbic system or emotional brain. That tendency causes your teen's responses in many situations to be more emotional than logical. So even if you initially try to keep your cool and respond rationally to your teen, his or her emotional reactions tend to trigger a response in your own limbic system. This can really test your capacity to self-soothe.

Another challenge to your ability to self-soothe can be how emotionally affected you become when you see your teen struggle socially, emotionally or academically. Witnessing your teen suffer the consequences of poor decision-making or inappropriate behavior can also be painful as a parent. No matter the reason, seeing your teen's emotional distress can be gut wrenching. As I mentioned previously that stress can cause a tendency to be too quick to rescue your teen, but it also creates intense emotions within yourself that, over time, may have a cumulative effect resulting in feeling down or more emotionally volatile. That vulnerability takes its toll on your ability to self-soothe and hence on your ability to respond objectively to your teen. Finally, if you are prone to any mood struggles yourself, having a teen can be an especially difficult period in your life.

In Chapter Two, you learned how struggles with self-soothing can cause regressive behavior patterns in your teen. Struggles in self-soothing also cause similar regressive behaviors in you. See if you recognize any of the following tendencies in yourself as a parent:

- Do you try to **avoid** discussing your situation because you feel ashamed and to blame for your teen's struggles?
- Do you **fight** feeling any responsibility by blaming others such as your spouse, ex-spouse, school, other parents, other teens, and professionals working with your teen?
- Do you try to **flee** from these emotions though substance use or other activities that numb these feelings or allow you to focus off yourself and your emotions?

If any of these behaviors seem at all familiar, or if you can identify other similar behaviors, these represent indications that it is time to rework your own self-soothing skills in strengthening them and developing new skills.

The process of reworking your own ability to self-soothe has direct parallels to how this occurs in teens. You may want to reread Chapter Two, only this time to see how it can apply to you personally. In reviewing self-soothing, remember that it develops first and foremost through gaining support by those you care about and trust. So actively reach out to those you are close to for support. Consider finding additional resources, especially if your primary support is also the co-parent of your teen as he or she may be just as emotionally stretched as you are. Reach out to friends. Seek encouragement from your church, synagogue, or other social groups. Visit a therapist. Find a parent support group. Parent support groups can prove invaluable as often parents in similar situations can understand and empathize in ways others can't.

Learning how to relax physically also boosts self-soothing. Find and use whatever healthy relaxation activities work best for you. If you don't exercise regularly, considering adding this into your routine. Some parents find going to the gym invigorating;

others participate in sports, or take long walks. Some parents also find relaxation techniques, yoga, or meditation energizing. Also, consider finding a hobby you enjoy, something that allows an emotional respite from daily stress. Remember: in seeking ways to relax and self-soothe, you are focusing on your own emotional health, but in the process are increasing your ability to be an effective parent to your teen.

The Importance of Meaningful Relationships

Your teen is not the only one who needs meaningful relationships in life. So do you! These relationships are crucial as they provide the emotional foundation you need to give your teen relational support. In providing this foundation, these relationships should be with people that accept you for who you are and who understand your situation as the parent of a teen. Finding these individuals isn't always easy. Unfortunately, there is often a crowd of people willing to give unsolicited and ill-informed parental advice. These judgmental responses by others often undermine your emotional resolve. They can even adversely affect your sense of competency. Do your best to politely avoid spending much time with these individuals. Instead reinforce your relationships with others who display the qualities of meaningful relationships in their interactions with you, and do your best to display these qualities in return.

Within these relationships, recognize that your relationship skills may also have regressed. Regression occurs due to the natural self-protective tendency to become more emotionally withdrawn or conversely more self-absorbed when self-soothing skills prove inadequate. Regression can affect your relationships by significantly causing difficulty in recognizing and attending effectively to the emotional needs of others in addition to your own. Just as with your teen, the result can be focusing too much on your own needs to the exclusion of others (becoming self-centered), or withdrawing to the point of not caring about anyone's needs (yours or other people's), or trying to overcompensate by hyper-focusing just on the needs of others in an attempt to avoid dealing with your own. These behaviors can create problems in relationships that, in turn, can undermine self-soothing even further.

Perhaps you are not too sure whether your relationship skills have regressed? If so, ask yourself the following question. At those moments when you feel overwhelmed, do you find yourself more demanding, less patient, and shorter emotionally with those you care about? Or are you isolating from them and no longer communicating with them? If either occurs, rework your relationships skills. Without improved relationships skills, you are losing the important mutual support that meaningful relationships provide and are limiting your ability to be an effective relational role model for your teen.

With this in mind, in addition to continuing your efforts to bolster your ability to self-soothe, also focus on reworking your relationship skills. Find the time and energy to invest in important relationships. Work on displaying the qualities that comprise meaningful relationships with others. If this seems overly difficult, consider counseling, which may include couple's counseling. Developing quality relationships will provide you the emotional fortitude and wherewithal to give your teen the relational support he or she needs. It will also allow you to deal effectively with a challenge that most parents of teens face—splitting that pits responsible adults against one another.

Splitting occurs when a teen doesn't get the answer he or she wants from one adult, so instead goes to another adult to get the desired response. Typically, when the first adult then questions the teen about his or her defiant behavior, the teen replies that the other adult granted permission. The result is often friction between the adults over the differences or split between their replies to the teen. The focus then usually shifts to the conflict or split between the adults, instead of on developing an effective unified response to the teen's behavior. The result can be inconsistent structure in the teen's life due to an erosion of the adults' relationship with one another.

If splitting is your experience, working on your relationship and level of communication with others in your teen's life can reduce splitting and make your efforts—and the efforts of the other important adults in your child's life—more effective. To prevent splitting, maintain quality relationships with your parenting teammate, spouse, your child's other biological parent if divorced (at least in regards to parenting), stepparents, grandparents, and other significant adult mentors in your teen's life.

The Need for Healthy Structure in Your Life

Meaningful relationships help center a person and provide valuable support and feedback in learning to cope better with stress. When relationships become strained, coping suffers. If self-soothing also falters, one's overall ability to remain centered, and thus to function successfully, is affected. For the parents of a teen, strained relationships and a lack of self-soothing can cause a regression in their ability to maintain healthy structure for both themselves and for their teen.

Perhaps the stress of having a teenager is beginning to create such a scenario in your life. See if any of these seem familiar:

- Do you sometimes forgo following through on limits and consequences with your teen because it seems like too much effort?
- Have your daily routines, such as getting up on time and keeping up with household chores, begun to suffer?
- Do you feel scattered and unfocused?
- Do concerns for your child begin to monopolize your life—not just your parenting, but personally across all relationships and activities?

If you answered yes to any of these, your own sense of internal structure has been affected. Faltering internal structure may show itself in other ways too, such as forgetting to do things for yourself and other members of your family. It may even affect your ability to adequately meet all of your obligations at work and in running a household.

If you recognized any of these traits, there is good news. Revisiting and increasing your self-soothing skills and refocusing on the quality of your relationships can help alleviate much of the stress that affects your ability to meet your responsibilities at home and on the job. In addition, it is beneficial to work directly on reinforcing healthy structure both for yourself and your teen. Pay attention to providing your teen with appropriate limits and consequences, making adjustments as needed. Ensure adjustments include retaining positive family routines, even if your teen seems to disparage these. Beyond your teen, also focus on reinstating and maintaining healthy structure in your own life, as that structure will make life easier and reduce your stress level.

In reinforcing your own personal structure, make sure to include retaining positive routines for your teen and those that provide enjoyment and relaxation for you too. Sometimes you may be tempted to forgo positive routines—going out to dinner, exercising, or going to a movie—but these normal pleasurable activities help keep you emotionally, socially, and physically healthy. If you feel tempted to skip these activities, remember that you can be the best parent to your child when you are rested, emotionally calm, healthy, and at your best. Maintaining these healthy routines isn't selfish; it is what makes you a better person and hence a better parent to your teen.

Reinforce Your Personal Sense of Self

Being the parent of a teen may affect more than just your ability to self-soothe, your relationship skills, and your capacity to effectively structure your life. It can also adversely affect your own personal sense of self and overall identity. Adverse effects occur when you begin to interpret your teen's struggles as personal failures. While likely you believe you have been a good parent in the past, when you see your teen struggle, you may question your competency as a parent. As a result, you may feel the need to try to hide your teen's struggles in fear of others thinking less of you as a person. You may worry that if others think you can't control your own child, then perhaps they will think you are out of control in other areas of your life. You may even begin to personally question how in control you really are in life. This self-doubting may make you second-guess your actions in parenting your teen and in life in general, making you less effective in both.

If self-doubt rings true for you, here is the reality: you remain as competent as ever! Only one change has occurred: you are being challenged as a parent in new, unpredictable ways because of what is happening in your teen's life. The challenge of raising a teen requires adjusting your parenting approach as well as revisiting your own emotional, social, and psychological capabilities. Even if you do everything right, your teen can still struggle because of peer and social influences in his or her life interacting with unique biological and cognitive factors. So strive to remain confident in your abilities by remembering that you have been a good parent, especially if you are reading a book like this. Don't interpret your teen's struggles as some kind of indication you are not a competent individual. Instead, move forward in life by becoming an even better person and parent—not because you feel like a failure, but because you recognize that it is time to build upon the strengths and competencies you already have.

Please note: You may need to address any mistakes or negative behaviors of your own that may be influencing your teen. Bravely owning what is yours can help your teen own what is his or hers. But in owning your mistakes, don't let the fact that you are human and therefore make mistakes undermine your sense of competency as a parent and an individual.

Final Words

If your experience of being the parent of a teenager is like mine, it is a wonderful experience. But it can at times be fraught with stress and emotional ups and downs. There is a lot to deal with and discover as a parent, including learning not only more about your teen but also more about yourself. The developmental spiral doesn't end with your teen; it continues with you as a parent. While this book is about supporting your teen's upward spiral developmentally, it is also about supporting your own. Embracing the fact that you are revisiting and reworking the same skills as your teen, although at a more advanced level, makes you a better parent. So I encourage you to reread the previous chapters with this in mind.

I hope the recognition that you are revisiting many of the same skills as your teen also helps you empathize more with your teen's struggles. Empathizing more with your teen may help you relate better to one another and improve your relationship. Why is this so important? No parenting approach can be effective unless it includes efforts to reinforce and maintain a nurturing and empathic relationship between you and your teen. Above all else remember to spend time with your teen, listen to him or her, and find ways to connect. Even when your teen seems unreceptive to conversation, your efforts to nurture and reinforce your relationship are having a positive effect. So keep trying!

Finally from one parent to another, I appreciate all you are going through. Being a parent is challenging, and being the parent of a teen is even more so. It requires you to learn new parenting skills and new ways of relating to your teen. It also entails working on yourself with the humility to realize that your personal development is also not yet finished. Most of all, it takes hard work, and lots of it. So I wish you and your family all the best. May your progress on the spiral of life be ever upward!

A DEVELOPMENTAL APPROACH TO TREATMENT AND ITS APPLICATION AT SUMMIT PREPARATORY SCHOOL

By Jan Johnson, MSW

An Upward Spiral is primarily directed towards helping parents understand and support their teen's psychosocial development. However, many adolescent treatment settings also use a developmental approach. Programs for teens often focus on these key areas:

- Self-soothing, often referred to as emotion regulation.
- Reducing unhealthy attempts to self-soothe (e.g. drug use, cutting).
- Building closer and more meaningful relationships with staff.
- Participating in fun, healthy activities with staff and peers.
- Developing cooperation, collaboration, reciprocity, and teamwork.
- Reengaging more positively with parents and addressing any conflicts.
- Increasing mature behavior through experiencing age-appropriate limits and logical consequences provided by staff in an empathic manner.
- Participating in therapy that encourages thoughtful consideration of the potential consequences of behaviors before choosing to act.
- Developing empathy.
- Volunteering and participating in community service.
- Learning to be more resilient in responding to peer pressure.

145

- Experiencing success in challenging situations that increase self-esteem, including through physical challenges that often serve as a metaphor for life's challenges.
- Learning to be more self-reliant.
- Learning to plan for the future.
- Being supported in finding out who they are (i.e. identity development).

So if you work in a treatment program, this book can also expand your understanding of how a developmental approach is used in treatment and hopefully enhance your effectiveness in working with teens. If you are a teen in treatment yourself, or are the friend or relative of a teen in treatment, this book can also help you understand the treatment process and what you can do to support it. To gain a better understanding of how this approach can be applied in treatment, consider the example of the non-profit therapeutic boarding school that my husband Rick and I started that utilizes the same developmental perspective presented in this book.

Rick and I, along with two dear friends, Mark Hostetter and Alex Habib, cofounded Summit Preparatory School in Northwest Montana, opening our doors to students in 2003. Rather than basing the program on the belief that some teens have a deeply rooted pathology or a worrisome moral flaw, we based our program on the perspective that the primary reason most teens struggle is because adolescence is a particularly intense period of psychosocial development. During adolescence, the psychosocial skills developed in childhood are typically too primitive to handle all of the new challenges teens face. When underdeveloped skills prove ineffective the result is childish, regressive, and impulsive behaviors. Our program seeks to address these struggles by helping teens develop more mature psychosocial skills, while simultaneously addressing any unique psychological, academic, environmental, or medical issues. The primary focus of the program is on helping teens get back on track in normal psychosocial development by learning the basic skills that all of us need in order to be well-functioning individuals.

A Normalized Setting

We believe that the best treatment environment for promoting normal adolescent development is one that mirrors, as closely as any treatment center can, the real world. Establishing a real world treatment program means giving teens opportunities to participate in regular healthy teenage activities and providing a setting that reprises similar academic and social pressures that teens faced at home. To this end, the teens served in our program are referred to as students rather than patients or residents. Our goal is to help teens learn to succeed in this normalized setting by acquiring new and more effective psychosocial skills. While our program does differ from most typical high schools in that we provide an overall therapeutic setting and twenty-four-hour supervision, we strive to provide a relatively normalized environment in the following ways:

- **A Safe Campus That is Not Too Isolated:** Like many programs that serve teens, in choosing a site for our campus we selected a location that provides a physical separation from potentially negative peers and sources of drugs or unhealthy pursuits. However, we believed that complete isolation seemed too artificial and restrictive, especially given the longer-term nature of our program. Because our average length of stay is fifteen to eighteen months, we intentionally chose a location close to a small, vibrant community in Northwest Montana, so that our students would not be separated from normal community social and cultural activities. From the time they enter our program, students are encouraged and expected to participate in staff supervised outings such as skiing, snowboarding, competing with other schools on our basketball or soccer teams, joining a charitable walk or run, attending art shows, going to movies, attending plays, and volunteering at a nearby nursing home, food bank, or community fundraising events.

- **An Inviting Campus:** A normalized campus to us means an inviting campus, one that purposefully doesn't resemble a juvenile detention center or a sterile hospital setting. We designed our campus to resemble a college preparatory boarding school or a small college campus, with similar amenities such as classrooms that include science and computer labs, an art room, library, student dining hall, lounge, gym with a climbing wall, weight room, indoor pool, soccer field, and miles of hilly woodland trails for hiking, mountain biking, and snowshoeing. The buildings are purposely designed architecturally to feel warm and uplifting with high ceilings and lots of windows for natural light. Use of stone and massive log accents are intended to convey strength and stability to students who may not always feel inwardly so secure. Students are purposely housed in dorms to assist them in learning how to interact appropriately with peers within a normalized adolescent social milieu, albeit supervised and therapeutic in nature.

- **Authentic School Experience:** For most teens being an adolescent typically means attending high school and preparing for college. Many of the teens we work with have struggled in their prior school setting. We believe the best way to work with these teens is to help them learn to cope with and manage real school, rather than avoid it. Our academic program does differ from many non-therapeutic high schools in that it is more individualized than most, has smaller class sizes, and employs teachers selected for their teaching ability and their personal commitment to struggling teens. But students at Summit Prep are still attending a real high school! The school is fully accredited by the State of Montana's Department of Education. We offer college preparatory coursework in regular classrooms that are teacher-led by state-certified instructors. We also have a special education instructor on staff and can facilitate academic support and accommodations for specific learning needs. This includes working collaboratively with a student's home school district if an IEP or 504 Plan exists.

- **Therapeutics That Aren't Office Bound:** Rick and I are both therapists, who very much believe that positive changes can take place through therapy. However, the usual hour in an outpatient therapist's office is not always impactful enough for adolescents who live so much in the moment and whose emotional perspectives can vary greatly day to day. Typically, waiting days to discuss with their therapist what just happened to them, how it made them feel, and why they acted the way they did doesn't always work so well. So while each student is assigned an individual therapist, the therapeutic aspects of our program extend beyond the therapist's office to the larger school and residential community. The community's combination of students, mentoring staff available twenty-four hours a day, and regular visits by parents and family members creates a therapeutic milieu where whatever interactions or group dynamics occur can be explored therapeutically. Inevitably, the therapeutic issues that students have become evident, which allows the therapeutic work to take place in the here and now. Therapy focuses on these real world interactions occurring within the normal daily routines of going to school, recreating, sharing a meal, or cleaning up together. To accomplish this requires flexibility in our clinical staff, including a willingness to work as much outside their office as in, and dedicated teaching and residential staff that prefer to participate actively with students rather than to just supervise them from the sidelines. Since we personally feel that interactive experiential activities are quite valuable, we also request that our staff be willing to participate in a variety of active healthy pursuits with students ranging from academic fields trips, cooking, knitting, and tending a garden to participating in challenge trips several times a year. These trips can involve camping, rafting, biking, or going on a volunteer service trip.

- **Parent Friendly:** Although there is often a considerable geographic distance between the teens we serve and their families at home, teens need their parents. This is normal and a fact of psychosocial development. Caring therapeutic staff can never replace how important parents are to their child, and that is not our intent. Our goal is to be a partner with parents in giving them the support they need for navigating their child's and their family's developmental path through their own unique upward spiral. As a program, we purposefully strive to be parent-friendly. If there has been conflict within the family, there may need to be a bit of respite or temporary time out between the parents and teen while communication skills are improved and trust repaired. But our hope is that the physical respite from one another will be of short duration, as the parent-child relationship is key to the psychosocial maturation process in teens. Family therapy sessions (by phone, webcam, or in person), family visits both on and off campus, family workshops and retreats, and eventually student home visits are a vital part of the program.

Emphasis on Empathic, Meaningful Relationships

Using a developmental approach also means focusing on the importance of relationships. Healthy psychosocial development occurs within positive relationships with individuals that consistently show compassion, authenticity, cooperation, reciprocity, and empathy—even when faced with the immature behavior that teens can often display. In our program, the formation of trusting and meaningful relationships is reinforced between students and their parents as well as between students and our staff. This requires hiring staff that are passionate about being a healthy mentor and role model for teens and who strive to respond to teens with a positive relational spirit. To accomplish this requires reinforcing the need for our staff to consistently implement limits and consequences with empathy and support, instead of with impatience or anger.

Healthy Structure

We believe that attending to the basic needs of teens reinforces self-soothing, and allows teens to focus better on psychological, emotional, and social growth. For this reason, healthy structure includes procedures and a daily schedule mindful of the needs of teens. Our daily schedule is crafted and regularly adjusted to assure that in addition to classes, therapy sessions, and therapeutic group activities, there is time for adequate sleep, physical exercise, recreation, and relaxation (yoga, playing music, reading, talking to friends...). Healthy structure also includes:

- A front office that is accommodating to students in helping them with everything from mail to travel arrangements.
- A kitchen staff committed to meeting the nutritional needs of students.
- A medical staff dedicated to meeting the medical and psychiatric needs of students that includes a school nurse and a child and adolescent psychiatrist as our medical director.

In responding to immature behavior, we believe that developmentally, teens still need externally imposed behavioral structure that adjusts to match their level of their maturity. This structure needs to include limits and consequences designed to foster both the internalization of self-limits on immature behavior and the thoughtfulness to think through choices rationally in learning how to make better decisions. So while rules and procedures are necessary for any program to run effectively, whenever these directly affect the students we serve, we are very deliberate in examining both their intent and the outcomes they produce. This includes behavioral expectations (such as acting respectful towards others), limits, and consequences. The primary goal of behavioral structure goes far beyond getting students to comply or making the job of our staff easier; it promotes psychosocial skill development and maturity in our students.

With this in mind we seek to provide rules, limits, and consequences that meet the following standards:

- Reasonable, age-appropriate, and rational.

- Continually adjusted to reflect the maturity level of students' behavior.
- Predictable, timely, and consistently applied.
- Applied with empathy.
- Designed to logically match the specific immature behavior.

Finally, healthy structure also needs to include engaging activities that staff and students participate in together. Be it hiking, playing a sport, creating a work of art, cooking, taking photos, or any other healthy activity, students and staff need to participate together both for recreation and also as learning experiences that encourage growing maturity. One example of this is our intentional use of outdoor wilderness-based activities to reinforce psychosocial skill development within our students. Easy access to the great outdoors through the vast wilderness areas of Montana is another reason why we chose our current campus location. Wilderness-based activities foster the development of the following skills:

- The ability to self-soothe through facing new challenges outside one's usual comfort zone, and through learning to trust others in accepting support in facing these challenges.
- Better decision-making by experiencing natural consequences for poor decisions (e.g. if you don't listen to directions in putting up your tent, you will get wet if it rains).
- Better relationship skills in learning to work together (e.g. the need to collaborate and to be mindful of the needs of others when navigating a raft together through whitewater rapids).
- The development of a sense of pride in oneself in having successfully faced a previously untried challenge.

A Program Framework Based on Progressive Psychosocial Skill Development

The Summit Model is built on the psychosocial maturity skills described in this book. Work on each of these skills is ongoing. It forms a continual spiral upward from birth through the adult life span (yes, even for us middle age and older adults). With this in mind we have developed a progressive system of stages for adolescents based on learning the key skills necessary to become a successful adult. Each stage has a series of individualized therapeutic assignments and activities, and when teens begin to show a **beginning** mastery of the skill related to that stage, they are ready to be promoted to the next stage. Here is a brief overview of each of the four stages.

Stage One: The Ability to Self-Soothe

This is the foundational psychosocial skill upon which other skills build. This skill involves the ability to keep one's internal anxiety in check, through self-reassurance when frustrated, so one can deliberate on a course of action instead of acting on impulse. Many adolescents have great difficulty self-soothing and cannot handle structure (e.g. cannot handle limits and consequences in response to immature behavior). Their response to frustration is to act rashly or to melt down in a fit of anger and defiance or hopelessness.

Stage One is designed to promote the ability to self-soothe by supporting our students in learning how to adjust to and tolerate, rather than circumvent, reasonable, non-punitive healthy structure. This is fostered primarily through students beginning to form supportive, trusting relationships with empathic staff that promote a sense of security. We recognize that developmentally the first step is just to tolerate healthy structure in a minimal way. We don't yet expect students to embrace this healthy structure in a wholehearted way. That hopefully will come later.

Because toleration comes first, at the time of enrollment into our program, we advise parents to empathize with their teen's struggles with the purposeful therapeutic structure placed on them by our staff. Our structure, although supportive and full of normal teen activities, can sometimes be in significant contrast to the level of structure teens experienced at home from their parents or by teachers in their former non-therapeutic school settings. We encourage parents at this point to focus mainly on reinforcing their relationship and the secure base they provide their child. Sorting through past problematic behaviors and conflicts comes a bit later.

Stage Two: The Ability to Form Meaningful Relationships

This is a skill that many times needs to be relearned in adolescence as relationships tend to be selfish and egocentric (often due to struggles with self-soothing), and people are treated as if they were objects to be discarded when no longer of use. Once their ability to self-soothe is strengthened, teens are able to begin to focus beyond themselves, and other people begin to mean more to them than just what they can do for the teen.

Stage Two is designed to encourage students to develop relationships with staff that gradually become meaningful enough that they are more willing to tolerate following healthy structure, including limits and consequences, for the sake of the relationship. This includes a desire on the part of students to be trusted by staff, which is why increased trustworthiness is one of the indicators used to determine if a teen is ready to be promoted to the next stage. In addition, students are urged to participate with staff in exploring and discovering (or rediscovering) positive passions and competencies they can build upon in life.

Family work also begins to take center stage and continues for the rest of the student's stay. Parents are key to a teen's progress, so this work includes family therapy, regular family visits, home passes, family workshops, and retreats. In addition, individual therapy begins to explore not only any personal issues students face, but also any unhealthy relationships.

Stage Three: The Ability to Internalize Healthy Structure In Life

Structure includes the perspectives used to evaluate if an experience is positive or negative and the parameters used to determine how to act towards oneself and others. Teens begin to internalize structure when they start to choose which qualities to incorporate in life through emulating the qualities they experience in their relationships with others with whom they identify (this is the beginning of identity development).

The focus of Stage Three is to facilitate success in our students by encouraging them to begin to internalize healthy structure by:

- Identifying with positive individuals (especially through the development of more meaningful relationships) including staff, parents, other adult mentors, and students.
- Testing out and beginning to incorporate healthy perspectives and behaviors through identifying more with these individuals.
- Beginning to demonstrate an increased ability to self-regulate by acting upon newly internalized healthy structure even when not in the immediate presence of staff or their parents.

Stage Four: The Ability to Begin to Individuate

The ability to individuate entails developing a differentiated personal sense of self. Beginning to individuate is important since, until this occurs, teens can be overly vulnerable to group pressure. Vulnerability to peer pressure occurs because teens initially equate their individual identity (their personal self) with the social identity (social self) achieved through contact with other important groups or individuals in their life. Teens believe that to be connected to these people, and hence to gain a sense of identity from them, requires imitating them. Remaining connected with others, while also developing a differentiated identity, is therefore difficult until adolescents learn empathy—in particular social empathy. Social empathy is the ability to empathize and connect with another person different from oneself without having to think or act just like them. This ability allows adolescents to also choose to be different from others and to establish their own personal values, goals and identity without feeling like this requires sacrificing important connections.

With this in mind, Stage Four focuses on students learning how to empathize in building close relationships including connecting with people different from themselves by:

- Exploring how those with whom they already have a relationship differ from them.
- Connecting with staff and students with whom they don't share much in common.
- Reconnecting further with parents and family in recognizing that differences don't have to impede close family relationships.
- Getting to know people with different backgrounds within the local community (through community service, volunteering, and participating in community activities).

Through these experiences students are encouraged to recognize that they can choose to be their own person—to individuate—without feeling like they have to be just like those they are close to. Instead they can selectively choose which qualities to adopt from those with which they identify. This also opens the door to identifying with numerous individuals with multiple perspectives in exploring what qualities they want to incorporate in life.

Resiliency is also a major focus in Stage Four as students test their resolve and ability to live up to their goals and values in life. This includes demonstrating the ability to successfully self-regulate even in the face of peer pressure. Resiliency is also encouraged through practice in being a leader, role model, and in handling more autonomy. Any regressions are seen as valuable opportunities to learn how to rebound. In addition, resiliency is reinforced through pre-planning by students developing a comprehensive post-treatment aftercare plan in collaboration with their parents.

To learn more about Summit Preparatory School
please visit our website at <u>www.summitprepschool.org</u>.

APPENDIX

COMMON TEEN DISORDERS

A developmental approach to parenting can give you insight into your teen's moods and behaviors, and provide you with parenting strategies for how to respond. Even when no disorder exists, these strategies need to be adapted to the unique needs and personality of your teen, and to specific circumstances your teen faces each day. However, if your teen struggles with an emotional, social, educational, or addictive disorder you need to also take action to effectively address it. Such a disorder can make life difficult for your teen, cause debilitating symptoms, and inhibit mature psychosocial development. This appendix provides a short introduction to common teen disorders and offers some thoughts to consider if you think your teen may be facing such a disorder. This appendix is not intended to replace professional consultation. If you believe your teen may have such a disorder, you are encouraged to seek the services of a therapist, addiction counselor, or psychiatrist.

Drug and Alcohol Abuse and Addictions

Drug and alcohol abuse in teens occurs for a number of reasons including unhealthy attempts to self-soothe or to self-medicate feelings of anxiety or depression. It also occurs due to the desire to fit in with a group of peers. Drug and alcohol use or abuse of any kind can be harmful to teens as it may result in teens placing themselves in dangerous situations (such as driving under the influence), cause adverse effects on brain development, and result in legal problems.

While drug and alcohol abuse can be problematic or danger-ous on its own, it can also cross the line into addiction. This oc-curs when use is no longer a choice, but becomes a psychological compulsion, which is reinforced by chemical changes in the brain especially related to dopamine (see Chapter One). When chemical changes occur, teens have difficulty controlling their use despite their good intentions to limit themselves and continue to use re-gardless of harmful or negative consequences. At this point, teens often become so preoccupied with drugs and alcohol that interest in other activities diminishes or ultimately use is incorporated into whatever activities they opt to participate in. Teens who are addict-ed find increasing difficulty in enjoying any activity without the use of drugs and alcohol. Besides a psychological compulsion, a physi-cal addiction can also develop. Indications of a physical addiction include the need for the substance to physically function normally, increased tolerance where more of the substance is required to achieve the same effect, and going through physical withdrawal such as nausea, shaking, and sweating when deprived of the sub-stance for any significant period of time.

If you think your teen may be abusing drugs or alcohol, or is addicted, his or her behavior needs to be addressed. Your approach should be calm and objective, and your focus should be on the be-havior and its effects, not on the character of your teen. Express concern, not anger, and reaffirm that you will not abandon them emotionally. At the same time, you also need to set definite limits on using behavior. For example, you may want to prohibit any substances in your home, insist on random checks of your teen's bedroom, require drug testing, prohibit your teen from attending parties where use is expected, discontinue any financial support that might be used to obtain substances, and institute strict con-sequences for use. Also, consider seeking professional help, as the potential consequences for abusing drugs and alcohol can be quite severe. A certified or licensed addiction counselor can assess the situation and help you determine how best to intervene with your teen. Drug abuse and addiction is serious because of the imminent danger it creates. In addition, further healthy psychosocial development is not possible if your teen has an active untreated drug or alcohol abuse or addiction problem.

Behavioral Addictions

Behavioral addictions are also referred to as process addictions. They involve patterns of behavior that teens initially adopted for self-soothing and/or enjoyment but that have over time become compulsive. To identify if an addiction has potentially developed, look for considerable anxiety and psychological distress when the behavior is not performed. Behavioral addictions can include compulsive behaviors related to such activities as gambling, sex, exercise, eating, Internet use, and shopping. Teens can be especially vulnerable to Internet addictions and eating disorders (which at least in part typically involve a behavioral addiction).

Eating disorders typically develop when behaviors surrounding weight, body image, and dieting become increasingly compulsive. They can result in such behaviors as self-imposed starvation called anorexia, a binge eating disorder, or a combination of binging and purging called bulimia. Sometimes excessive exercise to the point of physical injury can also accompany eating disorders. These compulsive behaviors are often fueled by an unrealistic assessment of one's own body (e.g. feeling fat even when significantly under-weight) and an overly rigid view of food and dieting. To identify signs that an eating disorder exists, look for your teen becoming quite anxious (sometimes to extremes called panic attacks) and depressed when not participating in these behaviors. Eating disorders can also cause significant medical problems. When severe, they can be life-threatening.

Internet addictions develop when participation in such activities as on-line gaming, social media, texting, gambling, shopping, or viewing of porn become more and more compulsive despite these activities causing increasingly negative consequences. Similar to other behavioral addictions, teens become quite anxious and depressed when deprived of these activities. They may also become highly resistant and angry when any limits are placed on these activities. For some teens, these Internet activities may also have become their main source of social interaction. For these teens when not a part of this virtual world, they can feel quite isolated and lonely.

While behavioral addictions are primarily psychological addictions, they also do have an effect on the brain somewhat similar to a drug or alcohol addiction. Participation in these activities results in increased production of brain chemicals, including dopamine, related to the sensations of pleasure. Over time, teens may increasingly seek the pleasurable brain states that these activities provide to the point of obsession.

If you think your teen may be developing a behavioral addiction, use a calm and objective approach in focusing on problematic behaviors, not on the character of your teen. Your teen needs understanding, not anger. Your teen also needs to know that you will not abandon him or her emotionally. Next, set definite limits on these behaviors, which may include prohibiting them altogether for at least a time. Also, seriously consider seeking professional advice from a therapist or psychiatrist. A behavioral addiction can become a very serious problem. The goal is the same as for any addiction: to mitigate it, so your teen can get back on track in life. Healthy teen psychosocial development is severely hampered if your teen has an active untreated behavioral addiction.

Mood Disorders

Every adolescent has ups and downs in life, however, teens with a mood disorder can have pronounced emotional states that either don't match or are excessive to the circumstances. Often mood disorders have a biological base that, when combined with environmental factors, cause extreme worry or fear, deep emotional lows, or unrealistic and manic emotional highs. Given the typical mood swings during adolescence, these can be missed. But if you think your teen is suffering from a mood disorder, such as anxiety, depression, or a bipolar disorder, take it seriously. If left untreated, a mood disorder can drastically affect the quality of life for your teen, may result in dangerous behaviors (including at times reckless or suicidal behaviors), and can be quite detrimental to psychosocial development. A mood disorder may also increase the likelihood of your teen developing an addiction if your teen chooses unhealthy, addictive behaviors to numb these intense emotional states.

So watch for signs of a mood disorder in your teen. Ask yourself, "Has my teen seemed emotionally down for an unusually long period of time? Does this mood shift seem more extreme than usual?" More significant and longer lasting changes in behavior, mood fluctuations, and general demeanor may indicate a mood disorder. Make sure to be open to discussing these emotional states with your teen in an empathic and supportive manner, and if you are at all concerned, consult with a mental health professional. Mood disorders in teens can be treated effectively through counseling, sometimes combined with the conservative use of medication. Mood disorders, if treated effectively, don't have to overshadow your teen's life and inhibit his or her psychosocial development.

Social Anxiety and Social Anxiety Disorder

Sometimes teens that struggle with social awkwardness also struggle with social anxiety. This is typically accompanied by the fear that others, such as peers, parents, and teachers, are judging them and are ready to reject them should they make a mistake socially. When the anxiety isn't too intense, teens typically can push through this anxiety if they receive adequate support by parents, adult mentors, and positive peers. Counseling can also be a significant help, including when social skill deficits reinforce their discomfort in social settings. If social anxiety becomes extreme, a social anxiety disorder may exist.

A social anxiety disorder occurs when teens experience such severe social anxiety that they become immobilized in social situations. This can be debilitating as often these teens begin to severely limit any involvement in social situations. They can experience panic just at the thought of an impending social activity. This rapidly becomes incapacitating as they begin to feel unable to go to school or engage in formerly enjoyable social activities. This can result in despair and depression, can increase the odds of drug and alcohol abuse or addiction, and makes these teens particularly prone to an Internet addiction as they attempt to find a safer social outlet.

If you suspect your teen has a social anxiety disorder, consider the suggestions given above for mood disorders. Often counseling, and in some cases the conservative use of medication, along with your support can significantly help your teen reengage with the world.

Attachment Disorders

An attachment disorder exists in teens that have a long history, typically from early childhood, of difficulty forming relationships with caregivers that they should rely upon as their emotional anchors or secure base. A secure base is the sense of reassurance, security, and confidence that children develop through a close connection with trustworthy and nurturing people in their lives beginning with their parents or primary caregivers. Through experiencing a secure base, children begin to develop and internalize the sense of trust and reassurance necessary to engage successfully with the world and with others. The lack of a secure base, caused by attachment difficulties, can create significant problems during the chaos of adolescence. In particular, attachment disorders affect self-soothing and relationships because the ability to focus beyond oneself in forming more mature relationships relies on the ability to self-soothe.

For teens with attachment disorders, relationships tend to be superficial as these teens struggle with empathy, trust, and intimacy. As a result, they tend to have difficulty maintaining friendships.

They may try to overcompensate by being overly clingy or prematurely independent. Behaviorally, these teens are impulsive, tend to be oppositional with parents and other authority figures, can be aggressive, and display little remorse when their actions offend or hurt others. Emotionally, teens with attachment issues struggle to cope and melt down easily under stress. In general, these teens also tend to have low self-esteem and a fairly pessimistic, distrusting view of others. Due to a lack of meaningful relationships, these teens also tend to be motivated primarily by external rewards rather than relational factors.

If you believe your teen struggles with attachment, professional counseling or treatment designed specifically for attachment disorders is advisable. In addition, being the parent of a child with attachment issues can be emotionally draining. It can create great difficulty in remaining consistently calm and empathic with your teen, which is what your teen needs from you. An important part of helping your teen requires keeping yourself emotionally and physically healthy, so also consider a parent support group or counseling for yourself.

Learning Disabilities

A learning disorder refers to a neurological condition in the brain that affects a child's ability to learn. In general, learning disorders affect how a child receives, understands, uses, and stores information. The struggles with information and leaning a child with a learning disorder experiences can take several forms:

- Trouble focusing on tasks and maintaining attention.
- Difficulty grasping certain types of information, such as computation concepts related to math or language concepts related to reading, writing, and spelling.
- Difficulty understanding how to produce certain types of information, such as organizing and composing written material.
- Difficulty understanding certain formats such auditory or vi-

sual information.

- Trouble processing information as effectively as their peers, including comprehending, remembering, and accessing previously learned information.

A learning disorder is unrelated to intelligence, but the roadblocks to success these conditions create can make an intelligent teen feel quite inadequate and not very bright. These roadblocks include such things as trouble reading, writing, listening, paying attention, speaking, or understanding certain subjects (such as math). Learning disorders are typically addressed by remediation and accommodations within the academic setting that supplement learning in ways that mitigate the effects of the disorder.

If you think your teen may have a learning disability, discuss your concerns with your teen's school. Consider having a thorough academic evaluation completed. This can usually be arranged through the school or privately with a psychologist. An evaluation will provide you and your teen's school with the necessary information to determine if a disability exists and what steps to take to address your teen's unique learning capabilities. This may include developing a specific learning plan for your teen, such as a 504 plan or an Individualized Education Plan (IEP). Medication is also sometimes recommended to help lessen some of the effects, especially of attention disorders. If the disability seems to be significantly affecting your teen's self esteem, consider professional counseling.

Nonverbal Learning Disorder and Asperger's Syndrome (AKA Autism Spectrum Disorder)

Nonverbal Learning Disorders (NVLD) and Asperger's Syndrome are neurological in nature. Both are considered autism spectrum disorders on the higher functioning end of the spectrum (which is how they are now typically diagnosed). NVLD adversely affect teens' ability to process primarily nonverbal information, many times occurring in teens that are quite adept verbally. This can include being good at verbal and detail-oriented tasks (such as rote memory learning), but having trouble understanding more complex concepts and in grasping larger patterns or themes. This adversely affects academic performance especially in higher grades. It also inhibits effective socialization due to deficits with processing nonverbal communication, such as not understanding the meaning of facial expressions or the use of sarcasm. Teens with NVLD can also have difficulty structuring their daily lives and adapting to new situations due to struggles with non-verbal problem solving.

Asperger's Syndrome has similar features to NVLD, but teens with Asperger's Syndrome tend to display more pronounced autism spectrum traits. For example, a teen with Asperger's Syndrome tends to struggle with adapting to new situations while also being quite rigid in his or her ideas and beliefs. A teen with Asperger's Syndrome may also have a fairly limited focus of interest (which sometimes includes an intense focus on one particular activity or subject). Behaviorally, a teen with Asperger's Syndrome also tends be more controlled and may act in a repetitive and sometimes compulsive fashion. This can result in the teen becoming quite anxious when unable to complete certain routine behaviors or to have certain favorite foods or items. Socially, similar to teens with a NVLD, Asperger's teens also tend to misread nonverbal cues and behavior. However, the social disconnect for teens with Asperger's Syndrome tends to be a bit more severe, showing more difficulty understanding and displaying emotions and creating connections with others.

Like all teens, teens with NVLD or Asperger's Syndrome need to learn to self-soothe, form meaningful relationships, and develop their own personal structure and sense of self. Although their developmental trajectory will be somewhat different, they will develop their own unique versions of these psychosocial skills. Here are just two examples of areas that require particular attention:

- These teens lack or have underdeveloped nonverbal communication skills. So learning many of the social skills that other teens grasp through non-verbal communication needs to be explicitly taught through verbal and written methods. For these teens, relational skills that most consider soft skills to be developed through experience, are really much more akin to hard skills to be taught similar to math or science principles. Social skills training that takes this approach is typically quite useful in supporting their psychosocial development.

- Teens with NVLD or Asperger's Syndrome struggle with change and a lack of routine. Predictable routines and behavioral expectations help them handle daily life and reduce anxiety. Predictability helps them self-soothe. Teaching them organizational and time management skills and assuring that they have a predictable daily schedule can help increase their level of confidence, success, and self-sufficiency. In addition, because most of these teens rely on routine and predictability, transitions can be very difficult. The more preplanning that is done—including what their new routine will look like and whom they will be interacting with—is time well spent.

If you believe your child has traits of a NVLD or Asperger's Syndrome, get a thorough evaluation, which typically includes a neuropsychological assessment. This evaluation will help determine if a disorder exists and how best to support your teen's developmental trajectory in becoming a young adult. If the evaluation determines that your child does have one of these spectrum disorders, learn as much as you can about it. Read books, go to lectures, and find a professional who can help. Understanding your child's unique way of experiencing and interacting with the world will help you better support your teen's upward developmental spiral.

Note: If you have a neuropsychological assessment completed for your teen you may see terms other than a Nonverbal Learning Disorder or Asperger's Syndrome used in the formal diagnosis. Although these terms are still in com-

mon use, they do not appear in the fifth edition of the Diagnostic and Statistical Manual of Mental Disorders (DSM-5). Instead, these traits are now classified either as an Autism Spectrum Disorder with a certain level of severity indicated and/or in some cases as a Social Communication Disorder.

BIBLIOGRAPHY

Arnett J.J., (1999, May). Adolescent storm and stress, reconsidered. *American Psychologist.* 54(5):317-326.

Arnett, J. J., (2000, May). Emerging adulthood: A theory of development from the late teens through the twenties. *American Psychologist.* 55(5):469-480.

Bowlby, J., (1999) [1969]. Attachment. *Attachment and Loss (vol. 1) (2nd ed.).* New York: Basic Books.

Cline, F., and Fay, J., (2006). *Parenting Teens With Love And Logic: Preparing Adolescents for Responsible Adulthood, Updated and Expanded Edition.* Colorado Springs: Pinon Press.

Ellemers, N., Spears, R. & Doosje, B., (2002, February). Self and Social Identity. *Annual Review of Psychology.* 53:161-186.

Erikson, E.H., (1994) [1980]. *Identity and the Life Cycle.* New York: W.W. Norton & Company, Inc.

Fricke, K. E., (2010, January). The Influence of Society on Queer Identity Development and Classification. *Vermont Connection.* 31:37-45.

Giedd, J.N., (2008, April). The Teen Brain: Insights from Neuroimaging. *Journal of Adolescent Health.* 42(4):335–343.

Gilligan, G., (1982). *In a Different Voice: Psychological Theory and Women's Development.* Cambridge: Harvard University Press.

Ginsburg, H., & Opper, S., (1979). *Piaget's Theory of Intellectual Development.* Englewood Cliffs, NJ: Prentice-Hall, Inc.

Mahler, M. S., Pine, F., and Bergman, A., (1975). *The Psychological Birth of the Human Infant.* New York: Basic Books.

Robb, C., (Reprint edition 2007). *This Changes Everything*. New York, NY: Picador.

Rubinstien, M.B., (2005). *Raising NLD Superstars: What Families with Nonverbal Learning Disabilities Need to Know about Nurturing Confident, Competent Kids*. London & Philadelphia: Jessica Kingsley Publishing.

Schore, J.R., & Schore, A.N., (2008). Modern Attachment Theory: The Central Role of Affect Regulation in Development and Treatment. *Clinical Social Work Journal*. 36:9-20.

Sicile-Kira, C., (2004). *Autism Spectrum Disorders*. A Perigee Book. New York, NY: The Berkley Publishing Group.

Siegel, D. J., (2012). *The Developing Mind, Second Edition: How Relationships and the Brain Interact to Shape Who We Are*. New York: Guilford Press.

Smith, A., (2006). Cognitive Empathy and Emotional Empathy In Human Behavior and Evolution. *The Psychological Record*. 56:3-21.

Stevens, Richard, (1983). *Erik Erikson: An Introduction*. New York, NY: St. Martin's Press. pp. 48–50. ISBN 978-0-312-25812-2.

Volkow, N.D., Fowler, J.S., Wang, G-J, & Swanson, J.M., (2004). Dopamine in Drug Abuse and Addiction: Results from Imagining Studies and Treatment Implications. *Molecular Psychiatry*. 9:557-569.

Walsh, D., (First Free Press trade paperback edition 2005). *WHY Do They Act That Way?: A Survival Guide to the Adolescent Brain for You and Your Teen*. New York, NY: Free Press.

W.C. Crain., (1985). Chapter Seven: Kohlberg's Stages of Moral Development. *Theories of Development*. Prentice-Hall. 118-136.

INDEX

Addictions
    behavioral addictions 85, 159-160
    and dopamine 15-16, 158
    drug and alcohol 157-159
All-or-nothing thinking 77, 89, 96, 102, 120
Authenticity 52, 61-62, 65
Avoidance 32-33, 35
Balance of Power 53, 57, 61, 65
Brain
    and addictions 15-16, 157-158, 160
    anatomy 12-13
    dopamine 15-16, 34, 158 160
    emotional versus rational 12-14, 135
    grey matter 11-12
    neurotypical and neuroatypical 16-17
    norepinephrine 15
    serotonin 26
    white matter 11
Bullying 20-21, 34
Chronic Illness 23-25, 25-26, 33
Cliques 19, 79-81, 97
Cognitive Development & Abstract Reasoning 51, 52, 56, 58, 77
Consequences and Limits
    (see Limits and Consequences)
Differentiation
    and entitlement 120
    and individuation 96, 104
    separation from parents 76

    parental need for 113-114
Disorders of Teens
    attachment disorders 162-163
    behavioral addictions 159-160
    drug and alcohol addictions 157-159
    learning 26-27, 163-164
    mood disorders 26-27, 160-161, 162
    NVLD and Asperger's 164-167
    psychiatric disorders 17, 26-27
    social anxiety disorder 161-162
Empathy
    cognitive empathy defined 95
    cognitive empathy development 105-106
    cognitive empathy and regressions 124
    emotional empathy defined 93-94
    emotional empathy development 105-106
    emotional empathy and regressions 124
    emotional empathy and self-soothing 113
    parental empathy 45, 86, 105, 110, 113
    practice with 117-118
    and psychosocial development 93-96
    and relationships 96
    social empathy defined 95-96

social empathy and individuation 96, 100-102

social empathy and intimacy 100-102

social empathy and moral development 99-100

social empathy and objectivity in parenting 113-116

social empathy and peer pressure 96-98

social empathy and reconnecting with family 104

supporting development of 106-107

and treatment 145, 150, 152, 155,

versus sympathy 93-95

Empty Nest 134

Entitlement Practice 118-121

Erickson, Erik 83, 101

Family

chronic illness or disability in family 25-26

conflict 21-23, 150

family routines 42, 140

family vacations 106

geographic moves 18

and individuation 102-104

and treatment 149-150, 154, 156

Fight Response 14, 15, 33-34, 35

Flight Response 14, 15, 34-35

Frankl, Viktor 116-117

Gangs 79-81, 97

Gay, Lesbian, Bisexual, Transgender 83

Gilligan, Carol 99-100

Groupthink

defined 76-77

and development 76-79

and friends 96-97

and identity confusion 81

and information technology 84-85

Heraclitus 5, 27

Identity

cliques and gangs 79-81

conflict with sociocultural norms 83

confusion and groupthink 81-83

defined 72-74

development 70, 71, 72, 74-76, 88

and entitlement 120

and groupthink 76-79

and individuation 88-89, 92-93, 96, 107, 118

and information technology 84-85

and meaningful relationships 70

and treatment 155-156

Individuation

defined 92

and differentiation 76

and the family 102-104

and groupthink 76

and identity confusion 83

and internalizing healthy structure 88-89

and intimacy 100-102

promoting 104-107, 118

and regression 126-127

and social empathy 96, 99, 100-102

and treatment 155-156

Information Technology

and groupthink 84-85

on-line gaming 84-85

and 24-hour connectivity 84

Injured Athletes 24

Intimacy 100-102

Invasion of the Body Snatchers 129

Khan, Genghis 38

Kohlberg, Lawrence 99-100

Leadership/Role Model Practice 118

Learning Disabilities 26-27, 163-164

Limits and Consequences
  and authenticity 62
  and balance of power 61-62
  and empathy 105
  logical consequences 88
  parenting challenge 134
  recommendations for 41, 86-88
  and structure 42, 44-45
  and treatment 145, 150, 151, 154

Listening, importance of 53-54, 57

Meaningful Relationships
  and abstract reasoning 51-52, 55-56
  and attachment disorders 163
  and authenticity 52, 56-57, 61-62, 65
  and balance of power 53, 57, 61, 65
  and cooperation, reciprocity 52-53, 59-62,
  defined 52-54
  and identity 70, 72, 89, 155
  and importance of listening 53, 57,
  learned through example 58-62
  parental need for 137-139
  and regressions 124-125
  and self-soothing 55-57
  and structure 63-64

and treatment 150, 154

Meltdowns
  avoidance response 32-33, 35
  defined 30-32
  fight response 33-34
  flight response 34-35
  nuclear 32
  and self-protection 32
  and self-soothing 30-32

Mentors 63, 107, 139, 155, 161

Morality
  pre-conventional and conventional 53, 99
  principled 99-100

Nonverbal Learning Disorders and Asperger's 17, 68, 164-167

Normalized Treatment Setting
  campus 147-148
  parent friendly 149-150
  school 148
  therapeutics 148-149

Nuclear Meltdowns 32

Parental
  authority 61-62
  empathy, displaying to teens 45, 86, 105, 110, 113
  example to teens 47-48, 105, 117-118
  need for meaningful relationships 137-139
  objectivity and social empathy 113-116
  over controlling behavior 113
  personal sense of self 140-141
  reinforcing relationship with teens 59-62, 116
  rescuing behavior 112-114, 126
  self-soothing 135-137
  stress and change 132-135
  structure, need for 139-140

Pecking Order 80-81
Personal Boundaries
    defined 73-74
    and developing a personal self
    92
    and enmeshment 65-66
    and groupthink 76
Personal Self
    defined 73
    and groupthink 79
    and identity confusion 81-83
    and individuation 88-89, 92,
    104, 155
    and information technology
    84-85
    and intimacy 101
    in parents 140-141
    and personal moral code 100
    and regressions 126
    and social empathy 96, 107
    and social self 75
Psychosocial Development
    in adolescence 9-11, 146
    and adolescent disorders 157
    and the balance of relation-
    ships and structure 47-48
    in childhood 9
    defined 1, 8
    and disorders 26-27
    and empathy 93-96, 105
    and family conflict 23
    and family illness 25-26
    and intimacy
    and parents 127, 132, 149-150
    personal factors affecting
    17-27
    and regressions 110-111, 121-
    124
    and relationships 48, 55-56, 59,
    116, 150
    stages of development 28

and technology
and trauma 18-19
and treatment 145, 152-156
Reciprocity 52-53, 57, 59-61
Regressions
    and cognitive empathy 124
    and emotional empathy 124
    and individuation 126-127
    and meaningful relationships
    124-125
    and personal self 126
    and preplanning 121-122
    and psychosocial development
    110-111, 121-124
    and resiliency 121, 127
    and reinforcing maturity skills
    124-127
    and self-soothing 124
    and structure 125-126
    transient nature of 122-123
Relationships
    codependent 65-66
    enmeshed 65-66
    lack of 68-70
    meaningful (see *Meaningful*
    Relationships)
    parental reinforcement 59-62,
    116
    and psychosocial development
    116
    self-centered 51, 56-57, 67,
    118, 137
    and structure 47-48, 51, 63-64,
    71-72, 85-86, 139, 153, 154
    unhealthy 64-70
Rescuing by Parents 112-114, 126
Resiliency
    and being a leader/role model
    118
    defined 111
    and entitlement 118-121

and overindulgence 120

and regressions 121, 127

and treatment 156

Road Rage 30

Secure Base

    and attachment disorders 162

    challenges to 39-40

    formation in childhood 36-37

    formation in teens 39

    supporting in teens 41-42, 59, 95, 102, 124, 131

Self-absorbed behavior 39, 56-57, 65, 67, 120, 124, 125, 137

Self-effacing behavior 56-57, 65

Self-Soothing

    activities to strengthen/foster 40-42

    and being self-absorbed 56-57, 67, 112, 120, 124, 137

    in childhood 36-37

    defined 30

    and delaying gratification 2, 35-36, 40, 55, 112

    development of 35-40

    and entitlement 118-120

    and meltdowns 32

    by parents 135-137

    practice in 111-116

    and regressions 124

    and relationships 55-57

    skills overwhelmed 30-32, 124, 139

    and tolerating structure 42-47

    and treatment 153-154

Social Difficulties 19-20, 68-70, 166

Social Self

    defined 73

    and groupthink 76-79

Social Skills

    increasing 20, 166

lack of 20, 68-70, 166

    and learning disorders 26

Splitting 138-139

Structure

    defined 36-37

    development in childhood 74-76

    internalizing healthy 70, 71-72, 85-89

    parental 44-45

    parental need for 139-140

    practice with 116-117

    promoting healthy structure 42

    and regressions 125-126

    and relationships 47-48, 51, 92

    tolerating 45-47

    and treatment 150-152, 153-155

    willingness to follow 63-64

Summit Preparatory School

    campus 147-148

    founding i-ii, 3, 146

    and parents 149-150

    program stages 152-156

    school 148

    and structure 150-152

    therapeutics 148-149

Sympathy 93

The Breakup 45, 63

Trauma 18-19

Trust, granting 62

Unhealthy Relationships

    enmeshed 65-67

    competitive 67-68

    lack of relationships 68-69

Upward Spiral 8, 35, 56, 76, 111, 121, 122, 127, 132, 142, 153, 166

ABOUT THE AUTHOR

Rick Johnson, MSW, is a clinical social worker with over thirty years experience working with teens and their parents. He has been a child and adolescent therapist, and the chief administrator for a number of psychiatric and substance abuse hospitals and residential based treatment programs for adults and adolescents. Most recently Rick cofounded Summit Preparatory School, a therapeutic boarding school in Kalispell, Montana.